Praise for *DAUGHTER*

"This memoir is more than the st... Scott-Ferguson pours her mastery of language, poetic prose, deep spiritual insights, wit, and intelligence into *Daughter of the Isles*. You will grow to know Alice better as you see the impact of the experiences that made her the incredible woman she is. And in the process, you will come to a richer, deeper understanding of yourself, as well."

–Nancy Parker Brummett
author of *The Hope of Glory* and *Take My Hand Again*

"In *Daughter of the Isles*, Alice Scott-Ferguson takes readers on a journey from her childhood home in the northern isles of Scotland to homes in Ireland, England, Germany, and finally the United States. From her strong roots grew a woman of purpose who championed the strength of women. With both prose and poetry, the beauty of family, the world, and her faith rise from the pages. The combination of goodness, grace, and grief that visits every woman's life is portrayed with honesty. Alice's determination to stay true to her core beliefs while adjusting her thinking in other areas was inspiring. In this book's pages, I found courage to face the complex feelings of aging. Thank you!"

–Janyne McConnaughey, PhD
author of *A Brave Life* and *Trauma in the Pews*

"In *Daughter of the Isles* Alice Scott-Ferguson provides an inspiring, adventure-filled journey. The reader will be transported to various countries and remarkable experiences all while watching her deepening spiritual formation and ministry to women. An unforgettable memoir."

–Amy Whitehouse
author of *Out of the Vortex: A Memoir*

"With her exquisite prose and poetry, Alice Scott-Ferguson takes readers on a captivating, poignant, and transformative journey. As we delve into her story, we become acquainted with compelling characters. However, she doesn't shy away from the painful aspects of life. One of the remarkable aspects of this book is the journey of personal growth and spiritual development. We witness her transformation from a passionate warrior fighting for women's empowerment to a serene and confident individual who finds solace in the finished work of Christ. We can all learn from the humility she displays in acknowledging the need for new perspectives on God's grace. This beautifully-written memoir will resonate with those seeking inspiration, spiritual growth, and a deeper understanding of what it means to be fully human."

—Fran Stedman
therapist and teacher in London, England, and co-editor of
Partnering With God

"*Daughter of the Isles* embraces the heirloom beauty of Alice's tapestry of life. Her story is enhanced throughout with her eloquent poetry that dances across the pages like the waves of her native Isles. Like the rolling of the of the seas surrounding her Celtic heritage, her championing of women is woven throughout her life's work. Alice shares her love of living a rich life as she seizes opportunities to thrive in every circumstance, while profoundly professing the empowering Spirit as the source of her increasing faith."

—Jean Petersen
award-winning author of *Kind Soup* and the *Big Sky Bounty Cookbook*

DAUGHTER *of the* ISLES

DAUGHTER *of the* ISLES

a memoir

Alice Scott-Ferguson

CLADACH
Publishing

DAUGHTER OF THE ISLES
©2023 by Alice Scott-Ferguson

Published by CLADACH Publishing
Greeley, CO https://CLADACH.com

All rights reserved.

Our gratitude to Steve Birrel for the cover photo. Find his work at: http://www.stevebirrellphotography.com/

Author photo by Kathy Burhop

Poems included in the text first appeared in the following poetry collections by Alice Scott-Ferguson, released by Cladach Publishing:
  Pausing in the Passing Places: Poems (2018)
  Unpaused Poems: Real, Raw, and Relevant (2021)

ISBN: 9781945099342
Library of Congress Control Number: 2023946383

*To my beloved father,
who taught me to love the written word,
the significance of history and its heroes,
and to ponder the wonders of nature;
the man who first showed me how to
champion the underdog and to respect
the worth and equality of women.
May you know, somehow, that
this book is for you.*

TABLE of CONTENTS

CHILD of the ISLES / 10

PROLOGUE / 11

GRATITUDE'S CHILD / 16

Chapter 1. VOICES of VISION / 17

The AURORA BOREALIS / 24

Chapter 2. The GESTALT of GEOGRAPHY / 25

The SIGHTS of the SEA / 32

Chapter 3. ISLAND LIFE / 33

LOST and FOUND / 42

Chapter 4. EDUCATION and EXIT / 43

WHO AM I? / 50

Chapter 5. CARVING a CAREER / 51

The PARACLETE / 58

Chapter 6. The CEASELESS SPIRIT / 59

AMERICA the BEAUTIFUL / 66

Chapter 7. ROCKY MOUNTAIN HIGH / 67

WOMEN / 76

Chapter 8. The WONDER of W.O.W. / 77

MISHPOCHA / 88

Chapter 9. GROWING GREATER in GERMANY / 89

REMEMBERING the RIDE / 100

Chapter 10. COLORADO HOME / 101

DESERT DESTINATION / 112

Chapter 11. DESTINATION: DESERT / 113

MONTANA GOLD / 124

Chapter 12. TRANSITION TIME / 125

LOVE SECOND TIME AROUND / 130

Chapter 13. MARRIAGE ONCE MORE / 131

LOVE THAT WILL NOT / 136

Chapter 14. THINKING OUT LOUD / 137

CARPE DIEM / 144

Chapter 15. TALE *of* THREE TATTOOS / 145

FINAL ANALYSIS / 148

Chapter 16. LEAVING OUT LOUD / 149

The OPEN GRAVE / 156

EPILOGUE / 157

The WIDOW / 160

POSTLUDE / 161

RECOMMENDED READING / 163

ACKNOWLEDGMENTS / 164

ABOUT ALICE / 165

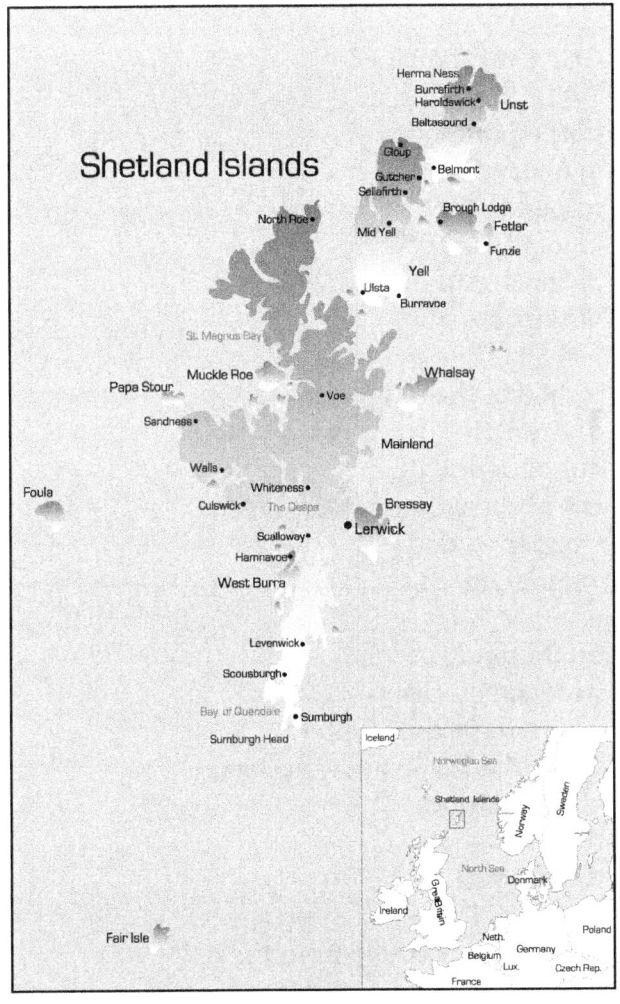

CHILD of the ISLES

bathed and birthed
in a womb of water
suspended
in solitude
distance and
distinction

a child of the different
of strength
out of deprivation
out of the water
wondering and
wandering

an unsteady youth
struggling to swim
where there is no water
with others who know nothing
of the distance
the difference
the distinction

a woman emerging from the
sea of solitude
takes her place in a world of many
bearing the wings of the water
the distance the distinct
forever a child of the isle

PROLOGUE

I have always loved men's hands. The combination of strength and tenderness intrigues me. As I began to write this story a vivid vignette emerged out of the mists of time—or more accurately, out of a heaving horizon of ocean—the surge of the sea at the mercy of the wind and me at the mercy of the oarsmen who manned the rowboat across an open stretch of tidal water. The four men with the oars defied the roars of the wild weather, their rugged faces set as steel as they navigated the familiar sea passage about half an hour from my tiny island to the larger Mainland.

Sometimes the sole, slight little passenger was a twelve-year-old girl being transported from her native, idyllic home to continue her education, a girl with a lifelong leaning towards motion sickness. Tucked under my seat was an empty milk can in the event I needed to upchuck—and more times than not, I did just that!

For holidays, for mail, for goods and supplies and all people transportation, we had to cross this sometimes rough stretch of water that was the sole means of transport to the Main Island, (simply called Mainland), before an airstrip and commercial airplane service arrived. If the weather and wind were right, then we went under sail.

There were quiet and gentle journeys too. But these magnificent mariners of those ferry boats never left shore without consulting the skies. Their strong, work-worn hands gripped the oars. The rhythm of the dipping, pulling and lifting—all of them in synchronicity—is still with me; I can hear the creak of the oars on the gunwale, feel the salty spray mixed with the tears on my face as I watched the beloved figures on the pier still waving till the distance was too great to see them anymore.

I put my utmost trust in those strong, caring hands and their knowledge of the moon's phases and subsequent tides. No GPS, no long-range forecast, no weather channel. They were mariners of the highest caliber and knew how to ply the water for safe passage. Nowhere in the annals of the ferry crossings of that day was there ever any loss of life recorded. Such trust served me well as I left my childhood and confronted a new world.

I respected men to the utmost. I learned from early girlhood to trust them. These were my archetypes for men of honor and integrity, those who put their own lives on the line for their women and children. At the same time, I was awash in an atmosphere of equality and mutuality between the genders.

The formation of this little girl who was to

become an ardent advocate for women's equality never suspected that for so many of my sister-women, such a stance would include hatred of our male counterparts. It would be many years before I discovered that not all men were as committed to my safety and success as those faithful seamen with the kind, strong hands, from an archipelago of those far-flung northern isles of Scotland—the Shetland Islands.

A SHETLAND SCENE

back, left to right: ALICE'S BROTHER, A FRIEND, ALICE
foreground: TYNE the dog

GRATITUDE'S CHILD

Gratitude gurgles up from the depth
of a satisfied soul

just basking in blessing of being
aware of the source; the stability
of knowing a Father who art in heaven
Who gives daily everything I need
Who can be trusted

Though my soul is severely troubled
thanksgiving wells and swells
tapping the spring of water from inside
that never dries
no matter how parched the ground

Anchored in the eternal ground of being
in the goodness of love
all is more than well
Faith and hope hook hearts
    and love is birthed

1
VOICES *of* VISION

My grandmother never heard of the self-care gurus Oprah or Deepak Chopra, yet it was she who, in a frozen moment of time, in a context long forgotten, leaned down at a family gathering and whispered in my girlhood ear, "You cannot love anyone else until you love yourself." Recently a friend made me a plaque with these words on it and signed it *Granny Nort*. That statement was a prophetic seed that grew in me as a life mission, to know and practice love, to learn how to value and cherish myself first of all.

Granny Nort was a product of the Victorian era when perfectly decently married women scarcely told their husbands, the father of their children, that they were pregnant. We never spoke of her proclamation again—which left me wondering where she had come up with such a profound conclusion. Of course maybe, wonder of wonders, she took Jesus at His word when He spoke something similar. For she was a woman of the Bible. The only other spiritual reading she had access to was the *Christian Herald*, possibly the sole print voice of evangelicalism at that time.

She was always Granny Nort (north) to

distinguish her from the other grandmother who lived on the southern part of the isle. I never knew her other than as a widow who lived with another daughter, my mother's sister and her family. She buried all her children but two, my mother and my auntie Tay. Long before I ever knew them, two of her boys died and were buried in India. They were eighteen and twenty-three, victims of disease contracted while in the Merchant Navy. I only ever knew one uncle, who became very dear to me, Uncle Alex. He and his family lived in England. When he visited he always brought me a pretty summer dress, and he would write me letters while he was at sea, telling me how special and sweet I was and that I would "do great things one day." I still have his letters in my treasure box. Auntie Mimie I knew and loved. I was captivated with her beauty. I felt her pain, though I did not understand the source, she whose nerves were wrecked from having lived through the Blitz of WWII. I recall the family sorrow when she died in London, so far away from her island home. Despite such desperate losses, my Granny Nort left this world singing "Jesus, Lover of My Soul."

Grieving was a color that I knew well in my young life. I remember women in my family wearing black for the first six months following the death of a loved one. Then the cloth graduated to purple for the remainder of the mourning year. I felt the weight. My young heart skipped and danced when I saw the floral frocks appear on my mamma, signaling the respectful and requisite days of mourning were over—until the next one.

Then there was my other grandmother, my father's mother, who we called Granny Mitty, because her house was called Midsetter. She had a spunky mind and huge heart inside a bent over body and sparkling Nordic-blue eyes which probably suffered any and every eye affliction from glaucoma to cataracts as evidenced by how proximal the newspaper was to her face. In later years she pored over the obits in the weekly island newspaper, wondering why she was left behind (as it turned out, she lived to age ninety one). She felt lonely for her peers and neglected by her God as He selected her to linger so long on planet earth.

She would always sneak me a coin or two to augment my sparse stipend when I would return to continue my nursing training. She sneaked because she perceived that her married daughter with whom she lived—my wonderful Auntie Jessie—would disapprove. I still hear the echoes of her mischievous laughter, as she poured me a tiny glass of sherry, filled to the meniscus, and declared, "*Drink doo up, itil no hurt dee, hinny!*" It would do me no harm, and it never did. I recall the warmth of the little libation lightening my steps as I bid her farewell—as always, wondering if I would see her again.

And my precious mom … the wisest of women, the bravest of women and the one who chafed under her isolated lot and many losses. Her father died when she was a young woman and by all accounts, she grieved his death deeply. She wanted to pursue nursing but, for whatever reason, her family did not permit her to leave the little island on which she was destined to live until her premature death at sixty from ovarian cancer. She was a caring, loving mother and wife. But she wanted more than the running of the *croft* (small farm) and enduring the long periods of absence when my father was gone in the navy or — later — on whaling expeditions, all in order to supplement the meager income that farming the land and the twin occupation of fishing, could provide.

Her voice left an indelible impression on me; though always the epitome of loving kindness, nothing masked her honesty and boldness of speech. When I joined her to peel the daily pot of loamy potatoes to cook for both family and fowls, she declared, "My *peerie* [little] lass, your hands were meant for better things than peeling potatoes." I felt a sting of rejection and wondered what better things I could possibly do. She meant it for good and, although she could not be precise about what better would look like, she had a dream that sealed my soul with promise and would reveal itself in time. That prophetic pronouncement made its way into the vaults of my heart ... tucking itself in alongside Granny Nort's grand declaration of destiny.

On another occasion my mother promised that "One day you will have a beautiful house of your own." This she declared in reaction to my insistent dedication to tidying and cleaning the living room for my parents' pleasure and comfort when they came in from working in the fields. I have known more than one stunning home in various parts of the world. That prophecy has been fulfilled many times over in the houses I have called home.

Most of the women were in the same situation, their men being away at sea for many months, and that is where I witnessed not only my mother's faithfulness and courage, but also that of the other island women, raising sheep and babies at the same time. During WWII she would clap her ear to the radio—which was always threatening to die from lack of battery power—to hear the list of the ships sunk that day. I would watch her intently and breathe normally only after she turned her face to mine, relief flooding her countenance, and declared, "Daddy's ship was not mentioned. He is safe for today!" I would run to bury my face in her apron, the smells of cooking and caring comforting my racing heart.

During the war my father's return home was always unannounced. I was sure I would always remember him no matter how long between deployments. "I will know my daddy when he comes home, by his white whoosh of hair in the front!" I can still see that figure opening the door and, sure enough, his white streak of hair was still there.

Another visionary voice that found a habitat in

my heart was that of the gentle, deep, and wise minister who would annually visit every home that had children attending Sunday school. I heard him report on me on one occasion: "Alice is a born organizer." (My brother was to know that trait as "bossy.") Yet another moment frozen in time and another affirmation of who I was. A solid foundation of inspiration, affirmation and hope was being laid word-by-word that would prepare me for a world far from my humble beginnings.

The final voice of vision came from my own childhood lips. When someone, observing my constant scribbling of stories, asked if I was going to publish a book someday, I quipped, without hesitation, "I will publish my first book at age sixty!" That was exactly what happened, though years passed during which I forgot all about the projection spoken that day.

How inexpressibly grateful I am. How weighty the impact of words to shape for good, or evil.

Deep down, from early years, I knew I was destined for a very different kind of life, although emotionally, it would cost me dearly to leave this safe and secure nest at twelve years old.

MATERNAL
GRANDPARENTS
HELEN AND JOHN
HENDERSON

PATERNAL
GRANDPARENTS
KATIE AND SANDY
SCOTT

The AURORA BOREALIS

Plasma particles burst
   from the boiling bosom of the sun
   on its faithful circuit of Earth.

Distorted and twisted magnetic fields
   appear, to our delight,
   as ribbons of the finest silk
   swirling in the northern skies—
   pinks and reds, blues, violets, green—
   dancing randomly in abandoned wild
   with crackling, crossing, swishing sounds.
Merry dancers I called them as a child.

The aurora is exhibit number one
   that ecstasy abounds
   at the Pole,
in the whole.

2
The GESTALT *of* GEOGRAPHY

Home! The furthest outpost of the United Kingdom. An archipelago of approximately one hundred islands slung out into the North Sea, 100 miles from the Scottish Mainland (of which it is a county), and 140 miles from Norway with whom there are strong ties as witnessed in the dialect, place names, and the strong shared relationship to the sea. At a latitude of sixty degrees north—the same as Anchorage, Alaska—the Shetland Islands are spared the severe cold and snow because they lie, in their pristine, beckoning beauty, in the track of the Gulf Stream, which superintends a maritime temperature. Not all the islands are populated. Those that are inhabited are similar to mine. For all of us, the capital town of Lerwick on the largest Shetland island, Mainland, was our seat of government, center of commerce, hospitals, police services, major shopping and continued higher education.

My little piece of treasured turf, two by three miles and twenty miles in perimeter, is called Papa Stour—commonly known as just Papa by those who called her home—an island of gently curved, sand-fringed bays, high cliffs, rolling heather hills and green, flower-filled meadows. The fishing fleet of long ago said the scent of the flowers guided them home to safe harbor. In countless ways, I was uniquely blessed with an idyllic childhood home where we were fully encouraged to be children, to play on the sands and beaches till the last ray of the sun, which in summer was for twenty-four hours!

With my mother's Kodak camera I snapped pictures of silhouettes on the beach as the sun barely dipped down over the horizon at one o'clock in the morning. The Islands are aptly given the appellation, "Land of The Midnight Sun."

In stark contrast were the winter sightings of the golden orb. Daylight débuted around ten in the morning and bowed off stage around two in the afternoon. Add to that the strong chance of clouds and rain, and darkness definitely dominated. Some have proposed that the populace of such northerly lands consider hibernating in the winter. But then the most spectacular of sights might be missed: the stars, so dense and bright and close that as children, we thought we could reach up and touch them; and the moonbeams that became the lovers' light and that still dictated the tides.

But most spectacular of all were the *Merry Dancers* (the Aurora Borealis) that swept the dark skies with silk ribbons of blue, red, green, and gold. With the neighbor children, my brother and I would dash out in the dance of colors, to the accompaniment of the crackling lights skipping through the sand dunes, lit up like a stage.

During daylight hours the rocks became imaginary villages and, with my friend Patsy I would play *peerie hooses* (little homes), creating families and stories of their lives, which amazingly enough was to intertwine with reality one day way out in the future where we would each have a child born on the same day, just as we had imagined in our play time.

The weather dominated and dictated activities outdoors, or not. We children spent endless hours among the shore's sea stacks (columns of rock) and on the pristine stretches of pink sand, but because of the chilly waters and unknown swirls of tidal pools, swimming was not a priority. What I loved most was the stream ebb where more of the world beneath the ocean was made visible. More of the mystery revealed! More rocks and seaweed, shells, and darting sand creatures—a larger world emerged.

It was our fathers' prerogative and imperative, not only to know the lunar cycles that determined the tides and informed the boat trips, but also to determine their children's safety by the shores.

There were sea birds aplenty. Cormorants and Gulls swathed the shoreline and sea stacks with their rudimentary seaweed nests and garnished the rocks with curtains of guano. Arctic Terns dominated the inland areas scraping out a mere dent in the shallow soil of the wild hills for their nests. During the laying and hatching season, their migratory presence was a decided deterrent to hiking as they dive-bombed to protect their young. My brother and I once rescued a lost baby Artic Skua and took it home. Until it could fly free, we cared for it and for several years after that it would return and linger on the land close by, letting us know it had not forgotten our care. We were so thrilled. Only much later was I to become aware of the science of imprinting.

The only other pet animals that we children were involved with were newborn lambs that the mother rejected for whatever reason. The little orphan would be taken home to be cared for by humans, and the *bairns* (children) eagerly became tender caretakers, feeding the lambs with bottles of warmed cow's milk. They bounced the bottle as if it was an udder and we had to hold on tight, as their tails wagged in delight.

While there were dogs and cats aplenty, they were utilitarian animals for herding sheep and catching mice, respectively.

Almost every croft had a couple of ponies. Not Shetland ponies—they are much smaller and decidedly much more feisty (even downright unpleasant) than their Icelandic counterparts. Icelandic ponies are larger and much more civilized. When the season of planting came around, the ponies were rounded up from those same hills to be harnessed for the plowing. That was the day my brother and I loved, as we got to ride the ponies home. We rode bareback, but gently, only allowed to ride as fast as a trot. I do recall that my brother was turfed off once, no doubt because he considered the equestrian endeavors too tame! I was to become an ardent horsewoman in my grown-up years.

Early life was interrelated with the land and the sea, small crofting and fishing and dependence on one another took supremacy over neighborhood squabbles. Sometimes a crew was required for fishing or a crowd of neighbors for the annual sheep shearing or bringing in the harvest. So, differences were dismissed, at least until such tasks were accomplished.

In a land of deep social divides, the inhabitants of the furthest outpost of the United Kingdom were deemed at the bottom of the heap, so to speak. Our speech was different. Our distinctive dialect was not considered a language as is the Scottish Gaelic spoken by fellow islanders along the west coast of Scotland. But it was for the most part unintelligible to the keepers of what we coined as BBC English. I grew up finding little to be proud of, or to boast of as far as social standing or status was concerned. That was the pervasive posture. We were poor crofter/fishermen from far away up north and "what good could come out of Shetland?"

Once, when a teacher from the Scottish mainland's children brought head lice into our little school, it served to pierce the prejudice and shed doubt on the belief that not all was perfect away from our shores. The horror my mother expressed and the torture my brother and I went through to rid us of the vermin, was an experience that lingers to this day. We were clean and careful and committed to our families and their welfare. Maybe we could start there to prove we were not less than.

When storms prohibited play and outdoor exploration, I would watch the power of the ocean from the safety of a warm home, through a rain-lashed window. Battering the shores, sending the gulls screaming upwards, the little boats at anchor in the bay bobbed wildly at the will of the wind. Fierce winds were forever a force to be reckoned with; a force that separated us from the rest of the world physically—a force of distance and distinction that carved places in my soul just as real as the relentless pounding of the waves that carved out the shapes of the stacks and moved the shifting sands.

CLIFFS

WILD WAVES

ON PAPA STOUR

The SIGHTS of the SEA

Blue on the bright days
   reflecting the sky
Gray on the dull days
   promising storm

Still and silent
   reflecting the shoreline
Roaring and cresting
   at the behest of the wind

Dotted with small boats
   plying their trade
Dipping with seabirds
   diving for fish

Lapping waves
   on the pristine sand
Laughing and sparkling
   in the summer sun

Morphing now
   in my memory as me
Flowing in my veins
   the forever sea

3
ISLAND LIFE

Every aspect of life was homemade. In the absence of the Internet and TV, reading was a major delight and source of knowledge. The schoolroom housed a small library, and there were those who read every book that came our way, my mother being the prime user. The long winter nights of those northern islands were fully occupied with reading, knitting, and music … and for me, writing.

The culture of music is strong in the Shetland Islands and our little island was no exception. My mother played the organ, a self-taught musician with an accompanying voice of a songbird. My brother showed his notable ability by playing guitar. (I recall a Christmas morning when he was very young that Santa brought him a little green plastic ukulele that launched his passion; I don't remember what I got.) My brother's children and grandchildren are all accomplished and performing musicians, as is one of my sons. Indeed, all my family has a keen ear for music of every genre. (I cannot omit the pipers and drummers of my children's father's family that contributed to their melodious bent.)

In my children, my mother's musical legacy is alive and well. Sadly, she didn't live to hear any of them play or perform. I followed in my mother's footsteps by playing the little pump organ in our living room and later in the church from time to time when I was back on the island.

It was well acknowledged that in this very active musical milieu, my dad could not hold a tune in a bucket! His forte was the gift of a photographic memory from which he could recite the longest psalm in the Bible—the 119th—and many of his beloved Robbie Burns' poems. It would be three generations on before I witnessed that spectacular gift passed on in the DNA to one of my grandsons. Another amazing legacy, along with my father's love of literature and philosophy, much of which I inherited.

The one-room school became our center of entertainment. The desks were pushed to the back and the floor cleared for dancing Scottish reels to the accompaniment of fiddlers and sometimes an accordion, and at Christmas time a stage was constructed for drama, poetry, and musical numbers that comprised our annual concert. Scarcely anyone was left out of the performances ... everyone contributed their talent. Simple, but bountiful meals, made by the women folks would be served to close off an evening of celebration. In the beam of his flashlight, I would walk home holding my daddy's strong hand, musical echoes pulsing in my ears all the way to bed.

Church life was fairly nominal, though it was the focal point for Harvest Thanksgivings, christenings, and funerals. The Church of Scotland was for the most part a very middle of the road entity, though there were some good, loving preachers who occupied the pulpit from time to time. Most people around me believed in God and knew Him as their source and sustainer and their judge to whom they would have to "give an account" at the close of the day; but a personal relationship with God was not in the prospectus. Others, like my mother, had come to a living faith through itinerant preachers who held Gospel meetings in homes.

When it came time for me to take my first communion simply because I was eleven years old, I refused. I wanted to commit to something and Someone real and vibrant, not merely go through the motions. Thankfully, my parents did not insist, showing their freethinking and distinction from most of the folks around them. My mother always went to the *kirk* (church), even when not playing the organ, and I would be nestled up against her scratchy Sunday coat, trying to keep warm and awake. A candy or two in the pocket of that Sunday-best garment helped to keep me occupied. I loved the benediction … which meant the service was over and we could go home!

There were other notable community

gatherings throughout the year, such as building the haystacks while the weather was dry. We bairns did nothing but run around the hay bales squealing with delight on a blissful, sustained, sunny day. The annual shearing of the wool of the renowned Shetland sheep was another day of gathering and a day to watch the brilliant sheepdogs in their glory. Children were merely in attendance to bask in the harmonious and happy work of the adults.

A not so happy event for me was the day of the pig slaughter. I would take off by myself to the farthest beach I could find so that I could not hear the squeals of the pigs. I would not have known what being a vegetarian even meant back then, but my deep sensitivity to all the animal slaughter—lambs, sheep, and chickens—set me apart and portended my life's journey. However, my mother was quick to apprise me of my hypocrisy as I relished the flesh cooked and served up in its delectable dishes. Some years would pass before I would resolve my dichotomy. For decades now I have been a vegetarian.

One of the major events for the island crofters was the annual livestock sale, called *Da Roup*. Everyone had their pens full of lambs, while the buyers paraded the cattle and calves round in a circle for viewing. The auctioneer barking out his rapid roll of numbers fascinated me. I was saddened, though, for the animals who still had a tortuous journey ahead, to the mainland, in a large barge. I think now of the stressful cortisol levels in their blood and that perhaps the renowned delicacy of Shetland lamb was not as healthy and pure as we all assumed. But the lasting impression from *Da Roup* was that most times the hard work was not reflected in the price paid for the livestock. I already knew that none of the profit from the many price hikes beyond the sale day, ever came back to the crofters.

Idyllic? Not entirely. It was hard for our fathers and mothers to make a living, to endure long months of separation from one another, and then to let their tender teenage children leave to continue higher education. Before my time, tuberculosis tore through the Islands and took the lives of many members of a family at a time. One woman, who was called Annie, became a legend. It was told that she would arise from visiting the graves of her husband and four sons and after drying the tears of sorrow, would walk back to the empty house singing a hymn of praise. Annie's story has haunted my heart all my life.

I was always aware that my parents wanted another life for me far removed from crofting and fishing, and even knitting. Knitting was a well-honed craft which brought in extra income. The island knitters were known for their colorful Fair Isle patterns and intricate lace shawls. These works of art were indeed fit for a king; in fact, every newborn royal baby in London received one such delicate shawl knitted by someone in the Shetland Islands. I did learn the craft, but not to the level of expertise of the island women of my family. I guess my hands were made for those "better things" to which my mother referred.

The idyll was real for a child, yes; but we could not but be aware of hardships, frustrations, and pain. Living on a beautiful island where the sun barely sets in the summer cannot compensate for the dark shadows that skulk year-round in every human heart.

MY FATHER WITH NELLY

THE CHANNEL OF WATER THAT TOOK THE
BOATS AWAY FROM PAPA STOUR

MY MOTHER AND FATHER
ALEX AND MARY JANE SCOTT

THE ORGAN IN
THE KIRK

THE SHEEP SHEARING

LOST and FOUND

Leaving the love of a place
beginning to brace for the loss
      of the silence, the space, the serene
      what will it mean to be penned in
      hemmed around
      by endless sound in the city?

Feels like pity
closing in on my soul
      my cry
      my 'why
      have I ended up here
      robbed of my cheer!?'

But there is more
I belong wherever I am
      There is more in store—
      lasting life hidden with God in Christ
      merely in another place
      living transcendently in glorious grace

4
EDUCATION *and* EXIT

On the island of Papa Stour, the primary—or elementary—education for the variable number of children throughout the years took place in a one-room school, with one teacher. During my early school years, there were about a dozen of us, and we came under the tutelage of two teachers, one after another. The first was an incomer, not native, and he brought with him his family, habits, and hubris. He was forever chewing antacids. Humorless, distant, difficult, he regularly fell asleep by the pot belly stove during class. It was then that some of the boys dared to rally us all to see how many times we could run around the building before he woke up. Not all the girls followed, though I always did. I remember the rush of excitement. And yes, we always got back before he woke up!

The other teacher came from a neighboring island. She taught us rudimentary French as well as all the requisite subjects, making learning valuable and to be coveted and pursued. I was an eager and attentive pupil. Mrs. Isbister was the wife of the minister who called me a born organizer. (I now wonder if I "organized" the other pupils at school as well?!) During my school years, many memorable and wonderful folks came to live among us. One dear district nurse gave me piano lessons.

We all walked to school from wherever we lived. For lunch I would go to my Granny Mitty's nearby house for lunch. There I would regale the family with stories and prayers, I am told. Already the preacher and writer.

Then there came the day that I made that sea crossing with a fully packed bag and an aching heart; the end of the long halcyon days of life in the bosom of a close-knit population of islanders. At the conclusion of primary education all children from the outlying areas and small islands were required to complete their schooling at a secondary school. Their destination was decided by sitting the eleven-plus exam which determined IQ and hence the school to which you would go. The topmost school, called the Anderson Educational Institute, was where this bright but broken-hearted little girl was bound for the next three years. And where she would perform far below her potential due to desperate homesickness.

I really was wounded and damaged by being separated from my family and made to reside with, but not embraced by, a very restrictive and unloving Christian home. I remember asking my parents if I could move to the hostel (as we named the dorms), but they told me that it would be very awkward to tell the family, whom they knew personally, that I did not want to continue staying with them; so that was the end of the matter.

Although the event left its mark of abandonment on my vulnerable young heart, I have never held any resentment towards my parents. My heart ached for them too and continues to hurt when I think of their dilemma, because not to send me to secondary education was punishable by law, and placing me in a home setting was their way of ameliorating the shock of separation from home into an unknown environment.

So, in the turbulent tides of pubescence, I left the haven of my home. I only returned for holidays, which were only Easter, Christmas, a week in October (ostensibly for potato picking, of which I did none!), and then the long summer holidays; but I could not get home for weekends because of fickle weather and the risk of being stranded, "storm-stayed," and missing classes. At that time there were no large motorboats, never mind an inter-island air service, which came much later.

A seminal story from this episode of my life further portended the woman I would become, the courageous warrior, the woman who demanded justice and fairness and was unafraid to pursue it. Each morning I would come down for breakfast and on my plate lay one listless, over-cooked fried egg, rather charred around the edges. I don't remember the toast but there might've been a slice, accompanied by a cup of milky tea. I sat alone at the large dining room table as the smell of frying bacon wafted from the little kitchen. My landlady cooked it for her children's breakfast and never offered me any.

After many weeks of this deprivation, I challenged her. This homesick, miserable little girl rallied under that banner of bountiful strong input she had been given as a child and spoke. "You are getting paid for keeping me and feeding me, and I want bacon too!"

From then on I got a rasher, not lashings, but at least one strip of the tasty treat. She uttered not a word of protest.

How I look back and love that little girl! The irony of this is I was to become many moons later a vegetarian with a particular passion for the welfare of pigs; so I never eat their meat now.

There was then a prevalent doctrine, firmly held by this family with whom I stayed, called the Parousia, or the rapture, as it became immortalized in books written much later. Jesus would appear in the clouds to whisk away the "saved." Now no young person in the world wants this to happen, of course; but during the agony of algebra class, I longed for that trump to sound, believe me.

That I did not succeed and live up to my potential was not surprising, for I was emotionally crippled in this environment, torn from my home at such a formative age and living in an unloving, non-supportive environment, all due to the secondary educational system at that time for the remote parts of the country, for which the Shetland Islands certainly qualified. There were no home-schooling facilities in place at that time, so parents had no choice but to send us away. I brook no blame. I am now grateful for the rigors and for the strength of character that it bred in me.

Students could leave school with a legitimate junior Leaving Certificate at age fifteen, which was equivalent to spending three years at high school. So I did just that and went on to pre-nursing college, which was even farther away from home, on the Scottish mainland.

LOW TIDE

PICTURESQUE CHURCH IN WEISDALE

SHORELINE STACKS

THE UBIQUITOUS BOATS

WHO AM I?

I AM...
A limitless edition
No partition
No separation
No daylight between
   the Divine and me

I AM...
United
No selvedge edge
Smoothly,
Seamlessly one
   with Triune God

I AM...
Connected
Created
A part of the whole
An irreplaceable unit
   in the Creator's purview

I AM...
Your sister
Your friend
Your enemy
From One Womb birthed
from a Force Field of Love

5
CARVING *a* CAREER

The Haugh, on the banks of the Lossie river, in Morayshire (in northeast Scotland) had been a monastery and it was converted into a residential facility for preparing girls for their formal nursing training. I continued to learn higher English, math, and literature as well as anatomy and physiology and other nursing related subjects. This gritty girl finally came alive. I was intoxicated with learning … a life-long incurable condition as I have come to experience. It was fun. I started to excel in all my studies. I was awarded the English prize and the Anatomy prize in my second year. I met girls from the Western Isles and from all over the north of Scotland. It was a two-year course and there were about twenty-four girls between the two classes. I became an avid runner and a voracious learner.

However, once more my finely tuned sense of justice was challenged in a most unlikely situation and an opportunity to fight for right emerged. The matron, or the headmistress, was vicious and unpredictable in her behavior, scary and mysterious to us all. I headed up a group that went to the education committee of the city and complained about her. She was discovered and diagnosed to be a heroin addict and summarily relieved of her position.

Homesickness no longer plagued me though home remained sweet, always, and I found my way to the jeweled islands of the velvet black night and of the endless light of summer days, on every break from studies.

Then it was on to the large city of Edinburgh, the capital city of Scotland, to do my formal nursing training. The ensuing three years were rich and rewarding. I was challenged and loved it. However, the tug at my heart's true calling would get my attention when I least expected it.

At one time, the then editor of the *Edinburgh Evening News* became a patient in the urology ward where I had a rotation. I was drawn to him like iron filings to a magnet. I wanted to know everything about becoming a reporter. He was thrilled. We were kindred spirits, but I was assigned to care for his condition, not write copy. Another beckoning reminder of the love of writing came in the form of the imposing Georgian buildings of the two main newspapers of the city, the aforementioned *Edinburgh Evening News* and *The Scotsman*. I captured them forever in my mind, looking at the buildings and thinking, *I wonder what they are doing in there? I would rather be writing bylines than emptying bedpans!*

I was ready to go on and do plastic surgery as a postgraduate course wanting to be different and break away from the predictable pursuit of most graduates, midwifery. However, a big *however* now hovered over my plans, for I was soon to encounter my own personal midwifery event.

I first met Jim, who was an undergrad engineering student, at a dance in the rec room at the Western General Hospital. From across the crowded room he saw me in my lavender dress with a pinched in waist and huge bunches of petticoats, as was the style of the day. Plus I had a lavender flower in my hair, which no doubt made me a compelling partner with whom to dance. Actually, he was an award-winning dancer, while I, afflicted with a paucity of rhythm in my feet, was no match for his moves on the dance floor! Such a disparity did not hinder our destiny, which was the start of a story of fifty-four years of life together. This was the young man I met and fell in love with and who became the father of our first child together.

In that day and era, becoming pregnant out of wedlock was a shameful thing. I had to leave the actual hospital in which I was training; but, blessedly enough, I had completed all classes required, though I was not allowed to stay on the extra three months until the board exams.

Such a situation horrifies me today, and the injustice of it never fails to numb me. I distinctly remember being assessed by the doctor who was designated to the nursing staff. He examined me with a very solemn face, permitting no joy to jeopardize his censorious countenance, only muttering minimal cryptic comments, after which I was summarily dismissed in disgrace and shame. It seemed like the career I carved had been gouged — but only temporarily. I later successfully passed the board exams and became a registered nurse. Such a proud day.

Now the little girl from the faraway remote island began her life in the same city, the beautiful capital city of Edinburgh with the young man who had fallen in love with her and their soon to arrive baby girl. Telling my parents that I was pregnant before I was married was an extremely painful event. My father embraced me and held me tight and until the day he died never spoke one word of rebuke or disapproval. Both he and my mother, indeed the entire family, adored my little girl with the golden curly locks—Sandra, their first grandchild. And her dad was inexpressibly accepted and integrated into the uncritical embrace of love. How could I be anything but a woman of compassion, confidence, and vision in such a field of light and love?

I loved Jim and Sandra both with all my heart and I devoted myself to the care of a little girl and to support my young husband who was finishing college and who always told me my day for further education would come when his education was over, and I knew that would be so. I did begin to take writing classes by mail, submitting articles to a writing school in London and getting my articles evaluated and graded. This set the course for what was to become obvious and actual many years later.

Another beautiful European city became home for our now family of four. Grant, our second child, was but three weeks old when we moved to take up residence in a little rental cottage on the rim of Dublin Bay, in the republic of Southern Ireland (Eire). My husband was privileged to study for his Masters in Electrical Engineering at the renowned Trinity College in Dublin. To live among the incomparable Irish, enjoy their wit and overwhelming hospitality was a privilege beyond words. Many years later I would return to teach at numerous venues in the country with the ministry team called Women of the Word.

Living in a predominantly Catholic country, more Roman than Rome, the role of religion began to catch my attention again. An Island nation steeped and sequestered in a branch of Christianity I knew little of, piqued my curiosity. Such devotion, and yet such division (an island divided into north and south purely on sectarianism), more than grabbed my interest.

At the same time, I was revisiting my own history as I was taught at school which made Oliver

Cromwell a hero in 17th Century Britain. But more accurately, he was a brutal tyrant denying the Irish Catholics food until they denied their faith.

I was consumed with washing nappies (diapers) and reading books that enlightened and illuminated my understanding of both history and religion.

I became more aware of the here and now of that war-torn land when I met the woman in Northern Ireland who wrote a letter of condolence to every mother in the south who lost a son to sectarian conflict.

The significance and prestige of the venerated Virgin Mary, the presence and predominance of a woman woven in the fabric of faith, was new to me. The elements of female (feminine) emancipation captured my imagination. I would learn so much more about that many years later. Something, Someone was stirring my spirit. My inner landscape was shifting as we left Ireland behind and returned home. When I observed my four-year-old daughter crossing herself at every church building, I knew for sure. Time to return to the land of the Reformation.

JIM AND ALICE IN PAPA

ALICE, THE NURSE, AT WESTERN GENERAL HOSPITAL
IN EDINBURGH

The PARACLETE

Teacher
of all truth unspoken
of things left untaught by Jesus
to elucidate what is already written

Intercessor
who prays perfectly
with unutterable inner groans
when we know not how to pray

Emissary
from the Father
as a descending dove
announced the Lamb of God

Comforter
never left the Son of Man
in the wilderness facing the foe
nor in the crucible of history, the cross

Advocate
birthed the church in fire
took up residence in and among us
sealed our place in the filial family divine
    secured our place in the circle of eternal Love

6
The CEASELESS SPIRIT

We arrived back in Scotland to learn that my mom was dying of cancer. The Comforter in grief, the Counselor in guidance, Spirit who has been with me since before I became incarnate on that far-flung Scottish island, took me down the corridors of time.

I was reminded of the little girl who prayed and preached at her grandmother's house during school lunch time, who was fixated on a painting in her bedroom entitled King of Kings and Lord of Lords depicting Jesus in the foreground of all the monarchs of the realm, and Satan a mere minion behind them all with a backdrop of hell's flames licking at his horns. I used to leave time and be suspended in timelessness for a few seconds. I did that often. I don't think I ever told anyone for fear they might not let me spend precious time in my room creating other worlds!

Now my marvelous mother was about to depart, the one who taught me to trust—and pray to—a loving Savior. Her loss was devastating to us all. She who had mourned the loss of so many, now left us to mourn her too soon; we were bereft of her beauty, warmth, and wisdom; she who carried the well-earned moniker of The Sage, stepped out of our space forever. My brother and I were still in our twenties. He married his sweetheart soon afterwards, while Jim and I set our sights across the Pond.

But first a short stint of work for Jim in the far north of Scotland, in Thurso, the closest town to the Dounreay Atomic Energy facility. Here our third child was born at home with a midwife in attendance. A baby brother for Sandra and Grant or, "A cat for me?" as his brother asked when he heard the first cry of baby Ross.

It was in this time frame that I procured a copy of the *New English Bible* with the intention of reading it as if I had never heard of Jesus before. Indeed he walked out of those pages pulsing with life and more real than I had ever known.

My husband also embraced a more vibrant faith at this time under the tutelage of a local Presbyterian minister, as did our little girl who attended a Sunday school run by the Salvation Army. You can't say we weren't eclectic in our sources. And maybe we weren't too discriminating, but the great Teacher knows the best way into hearts!

In a short time we were on our way to Rochester, New York. Jim was a recruit to the prestigious Xerox Corporation. When he called me from London at a physics exhibition some months prior about the offer to go to the States (in an era commonly coined "the brain drain"), I was ambivalent. I had unpleasant recollections of the "ugly American abroad" syndrome. The noisy, demanding tourists at local restaurants did not endear me to the Yanks. My response to the prospect of emigration was, "Hmm! Well, just for a couple of years." At the time of this writing, it has been fifty five … a long two years by any metric.

I had quite forgotten the following prognostication spoken into our lives some years before. Jim had been given a clean bill of health after contracting tuberculosis as a student, and we met for our exit interview with the chief of staff (in his elevated status no longer called Dr. but Mr.). From behind his massive oak desk, flanked with books on every side, he declared my husband fit and well with only one caveat.

Mr. Robinson said that the only thing we would never be able to do was emigrate to the USA. Such a possibility had never entered my imagination. Nonetheless this exit interview joined the file of frozen portends that turned out to be another wondrous working of the Divine in our lives.

Many years later emigration was a reality. Those telltale records were nowhere to be found, and there were, therefore, no prohibitions to our entry to the USA. With the well-worn vinyl of Dvorak's "New World Symphony" ringing in our ears and pounding in our hearts, we set off for that wide open space of opportunity, which would become the crucible of our lives and that of our progeny.

We left behind my grieving father—now a widower, which he remained until he passed away. But there were thirty years in between, so much more time and history to accumulate with my dear dad. He even came to visit us in Rochester. This was a settling time; a time of raising children, solidifying a career for my husband, and developing a life thesis.

We found ourselves in a non-denominational church and our hearts knit with a senior pastor who was of Scottish extraction and who fell in love with our little ones. And everyone, it seemed, fell in love with our accents! For many months there was not a Sunday after church when we were not invited to dinner at someone's home. When we joined the church, we slipped into the back pews. By the time we left five years later, we were right up front taking in the rich teaching and soaking up the love. There was a lady in the choir who looked and sang like my mother. I scarcely took my eyes off her. She never knew that the young Scottish lass in the front row was being healed by the sound of her voice.

Here my leadership skills were harnessed to team up with the assistant pastor in an evangelistic outreach, and in planning and running Vacation Bible School. My husband was involved in the audio-visual department and our kids continued to grow in the knowledge of the Scriptures and the love of their Savior. To this day,

I am still in touch with one of the girls I taught in junior high class. It feels like she is almost as old as I am now!

We partook of all the holidays (the Fourth of July was a new one to us) and the seasonal smorgasbord of activities, including grape gathering by the Finger Lakes, celebrating the Lilac Festival, losing our breath at the indescribable colors of fall, sweating in the unrelenting humidity of upstate New York summers, and then shoveling snow in the dreary, sunless winters. We became thoroughly American. Peanut butter and jelly sandwiches and Kool-Aid were just a few of the heretofore unidentified necessities of childhood life.

I wrote home to my dad with the shocking news that divorce was something that really happened here, and not just in Hollywood. I had discovered that the elderly gentleman who lived across the road was divorced—only the first of many I would encounter, of course.

Never has there been a moment we ever regretted that decision to emigrate; nor for a moment did we ever stop being grateful for our heritage. We made frequent visits back to Scotland, so our children would know what a cousin looked like!

Many years in the future, our beloved Pastor Crawford was to follow us to Colorado and be part of our younger son's wedding ceremony.

Ross's beautiful bride was the adopted daughter of a family near us. Her original home was the Philippines and it turned out that she had spent her final years there in an orphanage that we, at Brighton Community Church, had sponsored. I remember packing Christmas stockings for the little ones; little knowing that one of these precious children would one day become a part of my family. Perhaps one of the stockings lit up her eyes on a Christmas morning far away? Tears still spring to my eyes as I recall the photo taken of Tessie and the pastor together on her wedding day, she leaning her head on his shoulder. Such a recollection restores my wonder and amazement at the work of the ceaseless, seamless moving of the Spirit. You can't make this stuff up. It is so much more than we can ask or think or ever dare imagine.

ST. ANDREW'S CROSS, THE SALTIRE OF SCOTLAND

A SYMBOL OF FREEDOM, LIBERTY, AND PROMISE

AMERICA the BEAUTIFUL

Pilgrim from a more restricted place
to America, the parent
  of my progression
  land of my adoption.

Country of limitless opportunity
  for me and my progeny,
  ever grateful
  sometimes sad
  land divided
  in agony
  in greed
  in need
  of a re-birth of soul
  into a vibrant whole
  not of uniformity
  but of unity
  in our differences
  in our sameness
  with the world
  though still we hold
  that glorious space
  of being
  a framework
  of freedom.

Wide and wonderful land
  open your arms of welcome
  let us love one another
  let us not fear one another
  let us harness the love
  and discover fire again.

Let us trade our hubris for humility,
  thee and me.

7
ROCKY MOUNTAIN HIGH

In the days when I was baking cakes from ready mixes in boxes, I wondered who would ever bake a cake at 8,500 feet above sea level as was noted in the "high altitude baking" directions. I could only imagine a climber pulling out a Bunsen burner and endeavoring to bake a cake in the crevice of a snowy mountainside. When I moved to Woodland Park, a mountain town in Colorado, I then understood; for I was indeed at an elevation of over 8,000 feet. As well as observing the imperative of increasing oven temps and decreasing raising agents for successful baking outcomes, I found that running up stairs solicited a slowing down in order to ensure a successful adjustment to the thin air of a higher altitude.

We adjusted so well that we stayed for eleven years in one of the most beautiful states in the country.

It was a season of high growth and inhaling the intoxicating air of major milestones, achievements, and events. It was an era of unmitigated mixing in the life of a small community. Church life was simple and uncomplicated at this juncture of the narrative.

My husband's vocation was rewarding and his volunteer work equally so, from school board member to driving ambulances on his off time. How he thrilled to get the call, pop his red flasher on the dash of his car and zoom off to the scene of an accident.

But, that kind of schedule took its toll on family life, too. Not only were his working hours long, but he was also absent for much of his spare time as well. Many years later when our children were grown and coming to grips with their own "demons" he was quick to volunteer, in his own words, "I outsourced the raising of my kids to my wife."

It was the era in which men worked long hours to ensure that their family was provided for. It was well intentioned but flawed. The little woman at home was characterized as running a perfect home and producing even more perfect offspring. That it was not uncommon for those mothers and wives to be popping tranquilizers is now no secret. Mercifully I was not so tempted or afflicted.

School life dominated my days. Everything from heading up the Accountability Committee and parading our decorated float down Main Street in the wake of cowboy ridden horses and their odorous deposits on the road, to making costumes for the actors in high school plays; cheering for football players or wincing at the wrestling contortions of my sons in their matches, then roaring from the sidelines as the school band blew their horns and beat their drums at the local rodeo parade. All of that, and more. I loved it.

I was devoted to motherhood, and when I decided to return to the work world, I "interviewed" every mother friend who was also at work outside the home, about the ramifications of how to continue being a great mom as well as a working woman. I painstakingly advised my children of the change coming. One of them replied with the greatest grace and permissive release. "Mom, you are the best mother and the world needs you too!"

I was sad when, later on, the kitchen was no longer awash with the aroma of freshly baked cookies. Wonderfully enough, by the time my father came to live with us, he and my youngest were the kitchen gurus. I once even asked Ross for the recipe for the tuna salad he and my dad relished while watching "Little House on the Prairie" and "Star Trek" after school.

Then I returned to school. There was no reciprocity with my nurse's license from Scotland. I had to take psychiatry and obstetrics at the Beth-El School of Nursing in nearby Colorado Springs, both of which were postgraduate courses in my homeland. I met another adult student in those classes and we clung to one another as we cranked our rusty brains back in gear. She was also an immigrant from Scotland, and our friendship became one of the most treasured of my life. Though it was some years later, Moira was in her prime when she died. Memorable, and oft remarked upon, was our taking off to nearby Fargo's Pizza Palace for lunch where our stomachs were sated with comforting slices of pizza washed down with caressing Chianti. We were, of course, still solidly sober and able to continue afternoon classes. When we sat our board exams the following year, our Jims (her husband's name as well) drove to Denver to take us out to dinner. The restaurant was elegant and the menus long. After a day of selecting from scores of multiple choice questions, this proved too distressing for Moira. She threw down the menu in despair and exclaimed, "I can't make any more decisions!"

It was not a hard decision to choose my next stop on the journey. Human behavior is endlessly fascinating to me, so I chose to join the staff at a well known, private psychiatric hospital in Colorado Springs. It proved challenging in many ways. The patients mostly had the means to afford long term care, sometimes many years of residency. Medication, the mainstay of treatment, only permitted minimal group or individual therapy, where my certification in Reality Therapy (post graduate training) took second place.

I found it distressing that there was so little emphasis placed on practical prescriptions towards restoration for these patients. One patient had an anxiety neurosis so paralyzing that his attempt to obtain a driver's license was an agonizing, repetitive roster of failure. I offered, on my own time, to take him to the test and stay until he tried, once more. He passed. It was worth the reprimand I received from senior staff for my part in the success. I was to wonder more than once, why it appeared no one really wanted these precious people to get well and be as high functioning as possible.

When I entered the nursing profession in Colorado, it was the epitome of matriarchy. I often observed a subservient attitude towards doctors that was but a poorly disguised veneer of resentment, for indeed the nurses did rule the roost in their own manipulative ways. I was reprimanded on two separate occasions by the senior nursing staff for not kowtowing to the doctors: once for transcribing medications incorrectly from illegible doctor griffonage; and the other time for not picking up a bulging chart that broke open on the floor when a doc, writing his patient notes, dropped it. In both cases the physicians in question were fully aware of their actions and knew I was not responsible. In fact, from one of those men I received a glowing reference when I later moved on from that place of employment.

My organizing ability and sense of justice were readily triggered, and in this environment they emerged eminently. In an arena where mutuality could have been a model of males and females working interdependently, it was not so. In my day, more women than men comprised the nursing staff, and more doctors were male than female. I made every effort to model mutual respect but I think I proved too much for the system.

Much was positive. I loved my patients. And many of the nurses were gratefully emboldened by my trail blazing. I left with only respect for, and from, the psychiatrists.

Woodland Park in the mountains was a picture perfect place dominated by Pikes Peak in all its moods. Snow covered, mystically cloud obscured or sharply silhouetted against cloudless cerulean Colorado skies: this, our lovely dwelling place of peace. Though idyllic, there was no want of mental health needs in the community.

Under the auspices of the Pikes Peak Mental Health Center, another therapist and I opened a local clinic, which proved highly satisfying and successful. Edie and I were an energy to be reckoned with. We are still friends to this day. We treated patients with a plethora of pathologies, from domestic non-bliss to Vietnam War victims (whose woes were blamed on the effects of Agent Orange at that time before it came to be known as PTSD), to failing school children. The struggling students whom the parents brought in, were sometimes scapegoats for much more nefarious issues, such as incest or child abuse.

One case is particularly memorable as it did occur on my watch and subsequently brought the stepfather to justice and prison. Later, I visited him in the county jail. Sad and hard.

The victim contacted me many years later with the words, "Thank you for saving my life!" I am still in contact with that tender teen, now a grown woman, mother, and grandmother.

One fine afternoon I retreated to my mountain home, looking out at that great mountain peak, and flopped in a patio chair. A chat with my Lord was in order. It went something like this: "Take all that I am and have become, put it together and use it all in a new way."

In our eleven years in our mountain home, we had experienced the gladness of graduations from high school, college placements, and even our daughter's wedding. My husband now had an opportunity to return to the UK with a Defense Department assignment. We had one son left in school and he was, contrary to our expectations, eager for a change of turf.

So, preparations were set in progress and we sped back to the land of our birth, only this time it was to Yorkshire, in England—the country no self-respecting Scot should ever want to occupy! Oh, the enigma of God's ways versus ours.

COLORADO MOUNTAINS

COLORADO
ASPEN

HIGH COUNTRY PINES

A FEW
OF THE
MANY
MOUNTAINS
OF THE
MILE-HIGH
STATE

WOMEN

I salute you
    bone of my bone
    from that first rib
I exult in the brave ones
    ache with the hurt ones
    celebrate the successful
    who remain kind
I refuse to be anyone's political pawn
    degraded
    downgraded
    by any religion
We are enough—
    equal, yes
    but more mutual—
    That's how this world will work
As we take our noble place alongside,
    eschewing even a hint
    of victimhood
    We are good—
     Someone who matters said so

8
The WONDER *of* W.O.W.

Yorkshire! I have left much of my heart's DNA embedded in your soft, sweeping hills, rushing rivers, picture postcard villages and walled cities. I fell in love with a land of warmth, wit, and wonderful women. After that patio petition of my God to use all that I had become, I was briefly involved with a group of women in Colorado Springs called Women are Wonderful, just months before our return to the UK. The amazing Tina d'Azio was looking for helpers to recruit interest in her newly founded outreach, and I offered to make phone calls. That led to an invitation to speak at one of her Women Are Wonderful meetings; my teaching, entitled Anger and Depression, launched me into the world of women's ministry. I am deeply indebted to Tina for the opportunity to teach, and for the energy, enthusiasm, and reality of the Holy Spirit she injected into her ministry. Her vibrant and vivacious victory lap on earth was truncated by a serious illness that took her Home early: too soon, I always say in such cases. (Though how can I ever know if it is too early?) Fresh out of that visionary and stimulating experience of teaching, I took the fire back to my homeland, knowing not at all how that would materialize into ministry of any kind.

We rented some of the most gorgeous old houses in the most tranquil and enchanting villages in North Yorkshire. We began to attend a small local church called, more accurately, a Fellowship. The pastor and his wife were, as it turned out, fellow Americans. Although we were indeed Americans by choice, we were in that most privileged place of being dual citizens, and it was very, very good to be back "home." Ironically enough, when we were first contemplating our future, England was not in the running. Any place but England, said these fierce Scottish patriots. I am forever in awe of the Divine directives that move the heart to effect change. Those years transpired to be some of the most significant, fulfilling, and life changing in my entire life.

I was confident that I was to find a niche amongst those women of the Fellowship as a teacher. The leadership was eager and enthusiastic at first. I met women of talent, tenderness, and tenacity who began to emerge out of the shadows of some of the darkest and most oppressive patriarchy I have ever encountered. That this was the structure of this group, though, was not immediately apparent.

The leadership offered me the run of the entire countrywide cluster of this network of fellowships.

I would be a bona fide women's minister up and down the land—in their denomination exclusively, of course. To a lass freshly off the boat with nothing but a fire of freedom burning in her bosom, no openings and no sponsor, this was a most tempting offer. However, the decision did not take long: *No, thank you.* My commission was to be free and to teach freedom, so I cut loose and history was made. That we would have had easier access and more opportunities to speak had I accepted the offer, is probably true. But at what cost to integrity and conscience?

Women of the Word (WOW) was born out of the assembling of a few like-minded women, most of whom were from the Fellowship. They left under threat of spiritual peril. One wandered the moors in agony of mind, fearful of her destiny because she was leaving the covering of a leadership with whom the adherents had to consult for direction on even what kind of car they should purchase.

Our headquarters was in the home of Angela, a neighbor of the lady who wandered the moors. Ang became our able admin gal. She was the sole Catholic in our midst, the only one who knew anything about computers—which were, albeit, primitive forerunners of what we know now. Ang tore her hair out many times at our restrictive, narrow view of her gargantuan God. Decades later, after those early WOW days, I would discover I had more in common with Ang's concept of the Creator of love and largesse; it took Divine revelation to arouse my senses to this much larger Lord whom my beloved friend already knew and Whom I would come to embrace.

Her large, rambling multi-storied house by the river Ure in Ripon became the nerve center for this powerful and far-reaching ministry. Raucous and randy Yorkshire terriers of varying numbers always greeted us as we arrived. They unabashedly sniffed and humped one another frequently, which earthy expression of nature one of our prim and proper ladies found highly offensive. One of the team, who lived across the river, told me later, following our weekly day-long planning meetings, "I went home in a daze, mesmerized, and felt my head was bursting!" Dear Anna. She has since burst into glory, again, responding to the summons at sixty years young.

They were all such wonderful women eagerly embracing their inheritance of freedom, while learning to share it with many others. They were courageous and committed. My heart holds and enfolds them forever.

From this humble hub, the miraculous emerged. It is not even possible to capture all the details as to how we made the contacts, set up the workshops that fanned out over the land carrying a torch of freedom for hundreds of women. Some of the women who made up the team had latent gifts of teaching and preaching, which was awesome to see emerge. And so commenced six years of workshops up and down the UK and Ireland, with invitations to teach also coming from English speaking communities in Spain and Germany.

The zenith of this nascent women's crusade had to be the International Conference we held in the then state of the art Harrogate Conference Center. With not a penny in the bank we booked it and then went our way confidently trusting the Lord from whom we had already received such amazing openings. Months later we stood on the platform with a panel of speakers and musicians, looking out onto a sea of happy and hope-filled participants, in humble amazement at the gathering of women from as far away as Israel and Majorca.

A moving memory sums up my personal bliss of the entire event. After a season of rejection and harassment from prominent male leaders in the church community, I was bruised and buffeted and in much need of affirmation. One of our principle speakers, Jean Darnell, kept her gaze on me throughout the conference and I was ready to believe she too might be critical of me. Later she explained, "I was just loving you."

The message I taught was the one of freedom in Christ. The Bible was our trusty textbook, mainly the New Testament and in particular, the Epistles. The India paper pages were well underlined and every teaching topic color coded. From little village halls to large auditoriums the message went out: *You are free because God loves you infinitely and has gifted you magnificently!* (At this time it would have been impossible to believe that there were heaving horizons of revelation still to come into view; I thought I had a grasp on the ultimate).

Nonetheless they were glory days. They were halcyon days because we were happy, fulfilled, and peaceful. But they were also challenging and demanded very hard work. We were in the prime of our lives; indefatigable, effulgent, and enthusiastic. Even now, nothing that I have done in my calling or career surpasses the sheer excitement and enterprise of Women of the Word!

We traveled hundreds of miles, slept in strange beds (sometimes superintended by a blessed Bleeding Heart of Jesus statue). Not all the beds were comfortable, especially if we had to share one where the slumped mattress migrated towards the middle! We were fed well, and late into the evening, particularly in Ireland where meetings did not begin in the absence of victuals. More than once I had to politely decline until the teaching was delivered, lest I fall asleep in the delivery thereof.

The Irish taught us to laugh hilariously as they regaled us with stories of nuns, constrained convents, and peremptory priests. Some of the most tender and tenacious hearts awaited us across the Irish Sea. I recall one dear lady who, in her new-found trust in a loving heavenly Father, declared, "I am sitting by the phone waiting for God to call and tell me what to do next!" Some loving clarification was required.

And LOVE was forever the operative word. In our travels, those of us who were married left behind devoted and supportive husbands. They stood behind us in totality. Mine in particular; that beautiful young man I had married long ago in somewhat inauspicious circumstances, fully financed the ministry in so many ways. Yet another beloved man, my father, who lived with us, was irreplaceable in the vital keeping of the home fires burning and care of our various cats and the ministry mascot, Rabbie, the drooling, divine, Springer Spaniel who had endured six months in quarantine after arriving in England from the USA.

Rumbles of resentment came in many forms. Dissonance driven by jealousy just meant we pressed on and ran from it as the proverb pronounces. Not much else can one do about that little green gremlin! Most disturbing were the recurring collisions we would encounter with the "male headship" issue. From time to time we were sorely tempted to get a team of men who would endorse us, and put their names on our literature, and so silence the critics. Some of the team began to wilt in weariness over this vexing issue.

My objective was not only to show our confidence and authority as women appointed to lead and preach on our own, but to honor and respect our male counterparts. To garner a list of prominent male names in order to approve us in the eyes of detractors was, to me, immoral. Our goal was to free women in their own right, not to usurp the role of men. Equally, they were too valued to be used as letterhead that could calm the qualms of the doubters. The end result was that we steered our way forward under our own steam. We were always gentle in our insistence and resistance. We were forthright, resolute, and true to ourselves; surely the best demonstration of being a woman of freedom, worthy of respect.

We did take time to recreate. Refreshing weekend retreats in the glorious Yorkshire Dales and Moors were ethereal. Cramming half a dozen ebullient Women of the Word into a little cafe in the picturesque village of Muker was enough to make sure the only other elderly couple present would never return, we thought. We were assured later, however, that they returned many Saturdays following to see if those wild ladies (one being Ang with a rose between her teeth!) would come again. We brought such vibrant energy to the quiet little village tearoom.

We took long, wonderful walks by rivers, meandered the moors under a moonlit sky, talked into the wee hours of the night, on one occasion squealing in surprise and disbelief that the one who had been tasked with bringing sheets to our cabins had quite forgotten to do so. Now, how do we sleep serenely under rough, itchy blankets?

We would return to the fray full of ideas as to how to sustain self care. The answer to the question, at the end of a long evening round the fire, of *What does anyone do for fun?* was stunning: *Nothing!*

That is when I took the lead and decided to take horseback riding lessons in the village in which we lived. It was a decision of great magnitude that bequeathed me bountiful joy for many years. Others followed with less ambitious aims, but nonetheless significant resolves. Although not exactly a re-creative choice, for one woman, deciding to get her driver's license was a life enhancing determination and accomplishment.

Many years later, living back in the USA, I wrote my very first book, *Little Women Big God*, which chronicled the years of the WOW ministry. I would return to England for a book tour, an exultant event.

A lady took me aside at one tour stop and pulled out a crumpled note from her purse. She said, "You sent me this when my father died, and I have carried it with me ever since."

Where I might have expected her to quote some soaring words of profound teaching that had influenced her, the simple gratitude for a letter of condolence was humbler, but sweeter than honey to my soul.

From a prominent pastor's wife we had known, came a more ego-boosting bequeath, "There was never anything like WOW that set so many women free."

The woman whom Christ sets free is free indeed!

YORK MINSTER

THE CITY OF YORK

THATCH ROOF IN YORKSHIRE

MISHPOCHA*

Invite them all!
From every corner of the earth
Leave no one out

No color coding of skin required
Shades now morph into one blinding brightness
No gender gaps with which to grapple
Now a family of equity, amity and sweet accord

Every 'other' is there
No more adherents of a lesser god
That prayer of long ago fully answered
All in union and synergy with God and one another

This is God's mishpocha
His blood-bought family called to celebrate oneness
Bound with ties whose tendrils trail the earth
And run deep root systems to connect all hearts

Not one is lost

*Yiddish for *extended family*

9
GROWING GREATER
in GERMANY

Driving with the top down on my convertible on a rare stretch of English country road and an equally rare surreal, sunny sky, the cry rang out from the depths of my soul, *I don't want to just know more about You, I want to know You!*

The reply came swiftly and surely from the same center: *I will show you, but don't put me into your formulas.* The consternation and confusion that followed was significant, but the confidence that I was on a new path took preeminence.

The path began through the vineyards of the Mosel River Valley of Germany in spring and seeing the sticks that were the vines, pruned to the nub, confident that grapes would swell from the branches from which the sweetest of wines would be decanted. Come harvest, we would relish both the libations and copious amounts of accompanying rich food in this land of lusty appetites.

Meanwhile, it was pruning time. I heard the still, small Voice say it was the same season for me.

Pruned to bear more fruit, I recalled the scripture. I had no idea what that would entail, but I was about to discover both the promise and the pain over the course of the next few years.

We lived over two life-expanding years in Deutschland. Jim's employer was once more our travel agent. If you had asked me whether I was in love with "my" ministry or Jesus, I would have resoundingly retorted JESUS, of course. But rip it away, or as in this case, leave it behind in the UK to relocate to Germany, my identity emerged lucidly as somewhat more in love with ministry.

I truly did not see that my life and work was based on performance; that I was married to a meritorious system that was anything but grace. This was not all apparent at once, but the Great Teacher was at work, putting the people and events in place, fulfilling the promise to know God as opposed to knowing *about* Him.

WOW was wonderful; and, in retrospect, I should have closed its doors at the time of my leaving. I was letting go and growing wings to fly even farther than was yet in my purview to imagine. I was the paladin pronounced by divine decree, the call was my calling and apparently non-transferable. I regret that I thought my appointing someone as a replacement leader, made them one. And, the belief that a good thing should never end, which plagues so many ministries, became my regret also. The women I left behind were an irreplaceable team and for that I love and cherish them forever. But I quickly learned that they were not necessarily leaders. I flew frequently back from Frankfurt to Manchester until the mission was finally folded.

So, here we were. It was the month of November when we took up residence in an enormous bunker of a house in a small *dorf* (village) called Mengershied a few miles from Hahn Air Force Base, where my husband worked. We were tucked into the Hunsruck region at the confluence of the Rhine, the Mosel and the Nahe rivers. The gestalt was geographically gorgeous. A rich agricultural area where lush vineyards birthed luscious wine. Wine consuming became a pleasurable pastime and with the addition of partaking of the ubiquitous pork in all its many manifestations at table, I succeeded in putting on poundage, aided and abated by its cohort, menopause. The day I could no longer pull up the zipper on my favorite pants was the amber alert to the flashing red of weight gain.

Getting used to the monochromatic weather of a German November was grim. Short daylight hours, gray overcast skies hanging over great, gray houses. It always seemed cold. I missed England with a physical pain and I plunged into deep depressive troughs.

As was my wont in those days, I awoke early every morning to "do my devotions," but they were swiftly becoming rote and redundant. I had worn out many a Bible (falling apart Bibles belong to people who are *not* falling apart, or so I once believed). I had passages color coded in categories. Prayer was in yellow, for example. I knew it backwards and forwards, always the first one in a group to quote scripture and verse. Prideful devotion indeed.

So a new Bible was in order, one in as modern a translation as I could procure, and no more highlighting. "Jesus, I want to meet you afresh!" I cried.

He flew off the pages and floated my heart on deep and still waters hitherto not known. It was when I was scrounging through the Commissary Book Corner at the American base for that Bible, that I fell upon a book called, *Have You Ever Felt Like Giving up Lately?*. I devoured that little book and my husband came home to a re-surging wife again. David Wilcox's thesis was this: *God will deliver you.* Complete sentence, with no conditional clause. This was the first glimpse of unconditionality I had experienced in my Christian life. I wrote a letter to his publisher telling him what that book had done to transform and deliver me. I hope he received it.

Perhaps the greatest and most profound awakening was in my marriage. The outcome was fresh commitment to one another. "Lord, this crazy ride called marriage is your idea, so you live it out through our feeble and flawed containers." Super surrender in place! And our pledge to one another was to agree that there was no such word as divorce. We took it out of our vocabulary and vision of the future. Both these facets proved abundantly true over the remainder of our lives together; until death did us part after fifty-four years together. Mutuality was always our life; he was my most faithful and beloved supporter, and I, his.

The sky became ever brighter over life in Germany. Learning the language was a thrilling experience. My husband's school German was soon eclipsed by my newfound vocabulary as I soaked up the strange sounds at the *Sprachschule* (language school) and then the renowned Goethe Institute. I was on a learning curve of colossal proportions. I finally shared the thrill expressed by Mark Twain on mastering the German language: there is no thrill akin to finally getting all the verbs amassed at the end of the sentence. I remember the very spot on the road when I squealed that I had done likewise!

I'm forever indebted to my elder son, Grant, who came from his stint in Sweden (with his Swedish friend, Olle), for the encouragement and incentive to attend formal classes in the language. Grant, who has a propensity for languages, was of immeasurable help to his mother of much lesser ability. That I was in the lowest entry class at Goethe, and he and Olle the highest level, mattered not; we made the journey every weekday to the banks of the Rhine together, my fifty year old brain wired and humming with new synapses of speech.

Our home up on the Hunsruck was the gathering place for people from all over the world on the same mission of mastering the language. When we played after-dinner games, it was exciting to hear native tongues of Portuguese, Swedish, French, and English taking precedence over the German we were learning, as the parlance of discussing the best winning moves. German was not yet the tongue we could fully trust in order to win!

I also consider it an awesome honor to have met people from Eastern Europe whose second language was a vernacular German from their family of origin. We were there when the Berlin Wall came down, so the East was pouring into the affluent West and those folks of German origin were subsidized at the Sprachschule to learn their native tongue and become fluent. I recall the stories of the women from the Ukraine, who spoke of burying their dead, as all the men had already been killed or were away at war. Now these were strong women, who knew about interchangeable roles. To hear a group of those Ukrainian women sing a capella in a classroom of East German nationals in a class taught by a Czechoslovakian was an experience in cultural crossroads. I am so thrilled to have been a part of it. It was sadly obvious that none of the eastern satellite countries, such as Poland or Romania, liked their Russian fellow students. The rift was deep and wide. Broken humanity divided and distrusting of one another.

Then there was the girl from Malawi wanting to live in Germany who cornered me in the bathrooms one morning and told me, in English, of her many abortions; tears of anguish and regret and shame. Little did I know then how much of a portend that was for my passionate cause years later and up until now, for the unborn and the mothers in situations similar to that of my dear African friend.

Learning the mother tongue of another nation in which you want to live, participate, and communicate, remains one of the highlights of my long and full life. Beloved Brigette was such a light in those dreary *Deutsche tags* (German days) of winter. We met at a carol service in which the American Baptist church we attended—and a local German congregation—collaborated to visit a hospital. She looked across the group at me and simply said, "I am Brigette." At that time she knew about as much English as I knew German. We commenced weekly meetings at one another's homes in adjoining villages where we falteringly advanced our fluency in German and English. She loved the same Lord I did, that much we could communicate.

So, what did living in Germany add to my journey of learning or observing either egalitarianism or mutuality? For the first time ever I saw a postage stamp printed in honor of the *hausfrau* (the housewife). I put it in my memory box along with a piece of the Berlin Wall. Yes, keeping a spotless house is part of the German mindset. Watching a neighbor daily hosing down both her outside *Rolladens* (window shutters) and her boys before they were permitted into the house for dinner, pretty much persuaded me. I observed that women's wear was designed from the smallest size to the largest on the racks. And in the local swimming pools, every size and shape of female dove in and languished poolside in her bikini, no matter how much flesh could not be contained therein. I regarded that as advanced self assurance, which still seemed outside the grasp of their average American counterparts.

At the American church near the US military base, it was business as usual. Patriarchy reigned and to even allude to the fact that women were first at the tomb and last at the cross, created a backlash of historical proportions. Following a women's retreat where I was the invited speaker, I drove home with a monstrous migraine. The body language and disdainful demeanor from the leadership was palpable and poisoned my soul.

An American woman whose name I have regrettably forgotten, introduced me to a now defunct magazine, called *Union Life*. It sounded more like a train stop on the subway than what it was: a compilation of wonderful material written by the desert fathers and mothers as well as current writers, expounding on our oneness with the Trinity.

I reveled in these writings. Later I used them as

constant handouts in classes I taught. I even had the honor of having an article published in one of their editions.

Alongside *Union Life* I found another gem called *Christ Life*. I saw their advertisement in tiny print at the back of my *Christianity Today* magazine. It read: NEW COVENANT TRUTHS FOR THE NEW CREATION. That was me, I was coming to see! I later learned that advert was the only one they ever ran. I read it on a couch in Germany while in the slough of despair. My association with these precious people became a huge part of my evolving and coming to know my identity in Christ, and I am forever grateful. Again, I wrote regularly for their magazine and was affirmed and massively encouraged as a woman and in female leadership.

As the days in Germany drew to a close and we were packing once more, I hunkered in a corner of our massive, empty house and cried at the prospect of parting again. Brigette's observation was succinct, she who had seen me weep for England. "*Du hast nichts gelernt!* (You have learned nothing!)" A typically pragmatic German pronouncement! Crying and missing and longing for what was, is more than likely something I will never unlearn.

We returned Stateside minus my father who had lived with us in Germany. He, who would effuse with the village barber with only one word of German vocabulary, *Luftwaffe!* A man of his vintage and one whom he might well have seen across the trenches in WWII. He planted our vegetable garden and took care, once more, of our pets. He went back to The Shetland Islands, to the sea and the shores, the source of his essence—to the home of his heart. Our dog, Rabbie, the mascot, passed away in Germany. His remains, now one with the rich foreign soil that produced such lasting memories and mighty changes.

IN GERMANY

GERMAN SIGNS

REMEMBERING The RIDE

I well recall ...
the smell of the saddle,
the surge of the strength
the scarcely restrained power
the palpable excitement
muscles quivering in anticipation
unleashing the power
the pride of the ride
the becoming one
the morphing of rider and horse
       the walk
       the trot
       the canter
       the gallop
the thrill of the will
of two in tandem
terrifying, thrilling and free
thundering through the trees
under cerulean Colorado skies

Memories made with a friend
long absent from tethered earth
I fully expect her
to ride her five-gait steed
    in that celestial sphere!

10
COLORADO HOME

What and where constitutes home? My island home is certainly ground zero; but every place we lived we made home, and each home embraced us. Despite being a child of the isles, I've lived my entire adult life landlocked. The majesty of the mountains replaced the awesome scope of the ocean; both were larger than life and possessed the ability to hold my awe, respect and wonder of being a part of something grander and greater than merely me.

Returning to the USA again, we continued following Jim's career in defense, with his top-secret clearance and the subsequent secrets which he carried to his grave. He would always reply to the query of "What do you do for a living?" with "I could tell you, but then I would have to shoot you!" Sooner or later, we didn't ask any more.

We were to find our dream home in the foothills of the Rockies in Monument, just north of Colorado Springs with a view, on a clear day, of some thirty miles all the way to the Spanish Peaks in the south. Eight astounding acres of scrub oak and ponderosa pine for grandchildren and dogs and Easter egg rolling and July Fourth picnics on the gazebo ... at least that was the intent, but when the weather at just over 7,000 feet in Colorado dictated differently, we had to move the celebration indoors. Often it was not officially "summer" until the fifth of July.

These were days of weddings, new grandbabies and, sadly, in keeping with the normal stats in 20th Century American life, a divorce in our family, as well. Both my husband's and my own health were challenged. His high blood pressure became critical. And I was diagnosed with cervical cancer. I was raw and vulnerable and very distanced from the Christian lifestyle I had known before I left for Europe.

Upon succumbing to cancer, there were those who had walked with me before who now felt that their own mortality became too close for comfort as the venerated teacher/leader was attacked. For some, this meant the need to continue to defend the false gospel of never-ending good health; if you have enough faith you would never be ill. However, I had come too far along the spectrum of Light to have any doubts regarding my value and lovability. I had no doubt whatsoever that I was not being punished for sin or taught some lesson. Lessons were delivered wrapped in love and care.

Along with my complete healing from cancer, there was the emergence of healing of the distortions I had held of a loving God. At the same time as my body was ridding itself of the intruder, my soul and spirit were discarding erroneous concepts and uploading new data on the Divine, accruing information and revelation that was life giving, and it soon became evident that the new wine could not be poured into old wineskins. New paradigms proliferated, demanding new spaces in my soul.

Following the otherwise successful surgery for cancer there was the little matter of a large instrument being left inside my body. A twelve-inch metal retractor did not find its way out of my abdomen post surgery, creating a few baffling, brutally painful post-operative weeks until the alien object was discovered and then scooped out with another surgery.

On the upside, an out-of-court settlement compensation provided the opportunity for my husband to take early retirement and embark on training for emergency services, a "career" he cherished until his final illness. Meanwhile I began my writing life. The metal retractor, to this day, serves as both a paperweight and a weighty reminder of God's goodness, oversight, and promise of yet more life to be lived, even in the face of seeming mortality.

During the life of WOW, a notable publisher

in England contacted me to write the story of the ministry. I responded that I was too busy doing the work and I could not write about it. Now in the perfect setting and in the peace that settles after pain, it was time. I had zero computer skills at that juncture so the story began to be captured on yellow legal pads. How thankful I always was for my husband's exemplary electronic and technical skills. The story of the saga that was Women of the Word was published as *Little Women, Big God*, my first book. When, you might ask? Yes, when I was sixty years of age, just as prophesied, but totally unplanned and those fateful words quite forgotten until then!

Mothers Can't be Everywhere, But God Is was my second book. A title that I had promised myself to write many years prior, having grown tired of hearing every Mother's Day sermon positioning mothers as the ultimate gatekeepers of their little ones' lives. This was the direct opposite of what I believed. Such a title indicated that God was so busy or inept, He outsourced optimum child raising to the mamma. That little book's task was to dismantle such an outrageous notion. However, I noted with sadness that many young moms in the churches found this a threat to their firmly held belief, those for whom it was much more palatable to believe that God could not be everywhere so he made mothers. Ergo, reversing the maxim threatened their firmly held status.

The writing bug had bitten. Now, with a gal from my local writer's group, a co-authored book was born. A woman named Nancy, originally from Tennessee, was the definition of grace and goodness, of impeccable writing and, to this day, one of my most cherished and faithful friends. I had read her weekly columns in a local newspaper and fell in love with her whimsy and wit as she observed everyday life. When she wrote of the loss of her cat with such tenderness and vulnerability, her heart captivated me.

At a writers' conference sometime later, we sensed there was destiny in our encounter. That grew and continued as we attended our own local writers group and learned that we both saw the "women's issue" from very different vantage points. She was a classical complementarian, believing the man was the head of the woman; and I was not, and did not! Nonetheless, we became increasingly persuaded that we were being called to write a book together. And that we did, having pledged that if this project came between us as friends, we would lay down our pens. Gladly, that did not happen.

Many times I would read what Nancy had written as I began to write my thoughts on the chapter at hand. I would have to rise from my desk, get my balance and gather my thoughts, shaking my head muttering, "I can't believe she believes that!" But never did we put down one another's assessments. Our editors wanted us to get down and wrestle in the mud of dissension to give the book more appeal, but we refused. We were sure that we could make our point in eloquence and love. We presented a well written, thoroughly researched final copy and there was little need for much correction; except two notable exceptions on my copy.

The name of Rahab was not approved by our publisher to illustrate God's use of women in His plans. I made a vow to myself that whenever I presented my writing from this book, I would use my far away sister as an illustration of God's love and trust in the feminine gender. In addition, the reference to a glass of wine we indulged in after Nancy, the complementarian, had to jump start the car of the "liberated" woman who did not know how to use such a piece of equipment, had to be substituted with a glass of cool lemonade in the final manuscript.

Those two objections are indelibly etched on my memory. The sadness, frustration, and bewilderment still leave me aghast. It was permissible to lie and say we drank lemonade and to omit the name of a woman good enough to be on the honor roll of faith in Holy Writ and in the lineage of Jesus, but deemed unmentionable in a book based on diligent biblical exegesis to establish a case for opposing views of the vexed woman issue? Nancy and I bonded deeply in the process of writing *Reconcilable Differences,* though we did not persuade one another to move an iota from our originally held convictions.

Then I found Christians for Biblical Equality. They confirmed, affirmed, and widened my net in their exquisite exegesis of the Scriptures in this regard. What I officially learned through their publications and influence, was what I had always "known." I am eternally grateful to that organization. Later, when it came time to part company with a church community where my involvement was no longer tenable because of their stance on women, I made sure I had given some of these highly scholarly and academic journals to the head pastor for his perusal. When six months later he showed them still in his briefcase, unread (he admitted), I knew it was time to go.

Then I had an opportunity to become heard and involved in the voices that were loud at that time regarding homosexuality and AIDS by joining a group called Dialogue Dinners, where every category of sectarian and separated members of the community could be represented in an atmosphere of love and respect.

I truly learned techniques of hearing, listening, and responding in a way I had never before practiced. Along with one other couple, Jim and I were the token "Christians." Over the course of the years we participated, we shared fabulous food and deep discussions with Jewish folks, a lesbian couple, parents of a gay son, and affirmed atheists.

Colorado Springs came to be known as a "Christian Mecca," hosting many well-known Christian ministry organizations. One prominent organization spoke with an authoritative word on what was best for families in their relationship to God. Their predominant, pontifical stance was the impetus for these dialogues being initiated by those in the Christian community, those whose hearts found some of their stances to be unloving and decidedly ostracizing to the unchurched.

That same organization declined an opportunity to host an AIDS conference proposed by a visionary, public health nurse friend of mine. The disease was rampant at the time and lives were being snuffed out at an alarming rate. Her intent was to gather educated and experienced voices from around the country to inform the public and lessen the stigma associated with AIDS.

Tragically, in certain sectors of Christendom, those who contracted AIDS from sexual contact were viewed entirely differently than those who acquired the disease from blood transfusion. To me, that was a red flag for a fight. I joined my friend and we had a very successful conference, which we organized alone. Astoundingly enough, the large Christian conglomerate then wanted to take over the hosting of this successful event the next year.

It reminded me of the story of Nathan the prophet encountering King David—the story of the little ewe lamb that a traveling man with a large flock demanded of the poor man (in II Samuel chapter 12). I went to bat fearlessly against the brazen inequities explicit in this scenario. The patriarchy backed off with scarce grace. The grief of such events still explode in my soul.

On a much more tender note, I was arrested in the arms of awe when I heard a precious young AIDS sufferer say, "The day I learned to integrate my disease, I was at peace." To the ears of an erstwhile committed charismatic, that was a most alien aphorism. After all, we stood against all interludes, interruptions, and aberrant attacks on a faith filled life. It was another pivotal moment where grace and surrender to an awesome, trustworthy God was further magnified in my now enlarging heart, disentangling from censorious religion and patriarchy.

The certitude of my faith walk was unraveling, giving way to more mystery. I was aware that I had some miles to go on this journey of learning more. I was alerted to the inescapable fact that I was, more accurately, on an odyssey of unlearning.

ASPEN GLORY IN COLORADO

ALICE ON HORSEBACK

Desert Destination

From the wild open seas to the mountains,
    to round rolling hills and grand lakes...
    the desert now claims my presence, takes
    my heart in this last gift of time...
                          before the wakes.

Golden years like soaring saguaros, like
    communion coronets reaching for the sky,
    transcendent thoughts commune on high,
    join nature's praise of surrender and joy...
                          until I can fly.

As wondrous wildflowers defy depiction
    drape barren mountains in spring,
    there where blossoms least expected to cling,
    from out of life's losses and longing...
                          flowers still sing.

Perpetual sunshine, wrap around bliss
    of warm winter temperatures, soft and sweet,
    contrast to the desert held hostage to heat
    of summer from which there is no retreat...
                          ultimate metaphor for life itself.

11
DESTINATION: DESERT

The month of March is a mirage of flowers in the desert. After a rainy winter the flowers fill the spaces in between the hostile terrain of rocks that bake in roasting summer heat. We arrived in the Valley of the Sun, in Phoenix, in such a month. We were to hike every path and explore every mountain around the city in the years to come, but more importantly, it was the garden where our other family grew. We moved there, where our younger son and his wife and our three little grandsons lived. With those grand boys our lives were to be inexorably entwined, as both parents had to work outside the home.

My husband's retirement and our attendant chronology colluded to call us away from shoveling snow. For someone who grew up surrounded by the ocean, I was continuously curious as to why I did not want to live closer to the sea at any time in my married life. We both visited the beaches around the country and loved strolling the sands and leaning into the ocean breezes whipping our hair. No doubt it was mainly due to our children's choice of destinations and our desire to be proximal to them and our beautiful grandbabies. So, from the majestic mountains of Colorado we headed to the Desert Southwest. Contrary to the estimation of a native Coloradan, we discovered that there are mountains in the desert as well! We had so much fun exploring the hiking trails around the city of Phoenix, long before we discovered the rest of the unique contribution to scenery in the awesome, diverse state of Arizona.

Tearing ourselves away from our Colorado family and our gorgeous home of thirteen years, where major life events dominated the calendar of our residence, was excruciating. Every inch of that soil was part of our very DNA, the unsurpassable views forever etched in our minds. The Colorado babies had outgrown sleepovers and endless hours of play in the woodlands surrounding us. Now it was time to go and become a part of our other grandchildren's lives. And of course, as in Colorado, we remained deeply involved with our own grown children. I often declared to them that a grandparent's relationship is a vector and requires no mediation from their parents. To be at odds with my own children could never interrupt my relationship with the grandchildren. Thankfully there never was such a scenario to settle.

While my husband followed a retirement path that satisfied his heart of caring and rescuing the wounded and mangled by working with the Fire and Rescue crews, I was inevitably drawn to offer my teaching gift to the women of the church we had joined. We became members, yes, but not with great gusto. I knew from the outset that women were not honored in their fullness; men ruled, but once more there was a much bigger plan afoot that I knew nothing of. I attended one of the ladies classes taught by a gal who would become a very good friend. I sat under her tutelage for about a year, committed to pay my dues, as it were. I wanted to honor the leadership and gain respect as a pew warmer before I approached anyone regarding holding my own class on those Tuesday mornings.

I was enthusiastically welcomed at first. I enjoyed about six years of teaching great and growing classes of eager, devoted, delightful women. I began with one of my own created studies on the book of Job (what a wonder that anyone attended!). These were wondrous times. I held classes mornings and evenings and all seemed calm. The materials for proposed study always had to pass through the portal of the executive pastor. Even a life-changing class on experiencing the Trinity made it through the grail with an oblique compliment about my courage to teach such a weighty topic.

I would not want to leave the impression that there were not warm and gracious men among the leadership, but there were also dozens of encounters that solidified my alienation from the patriarchy and its prevailing lordship over women, along with woefully inadequate exegesis of the Bible. I was increasingly interpreting the Bible differently when framed in the love and value God has for all His people, His creation, and His universe.

I welcomed the rare encounters with pastors and teachers who would engage me long enough for me to ask the reasons they saw women the way they did. Their answers were built on "pull quotes," mainly from the Epistles referencing the role of women and interpreted as lower status. I once inquired what happened to the expositional "law of first mention"? In this case, the mutuality of our first parents, Adam and Eve, made in the imago dei, both male and female. Why would this mention be exchanged for those other less substantiated New Testament mentions? I was told that his particular seminary built their case on the "pull quotes."

The end of my affiliation at this church would come at the hands of one particular pastor who began to question my doctrinal position regarding the inclusion of all in the atoning work of Christ (on top of the women issue). My sources for all the studies were from impeccable academics in the reformed tradition, but he was unable to accept this grand embrace. The die was cast. The invitation to be the Women's Annual Retreat speaker was in grave jeopardy of being recanted, but by then my reputation among the women was solid and one of being trustworthy.

My magnetic north was ever the words bestowed on me by my prophetic grandmother. This commitment to cement that I was loved by my God so that I could, without mawkish mantras, love myself and pass that on to my students, was paramount. That, by definition, included the indisputable fact that women are not inferior to men. That was certainly not a welcome conversation and was not encouraged, indeed would not be entertained at the higher levels of many churches.

I had been faithful not to teach directly on egalitarian issues, but after one evening class I drove home with a sword in my heart. The weighty words of a student ringing in my ears: "When are you going to teach us about these things?" I knew that it was time to take out the oars and row my boat in another direction. To give the metaphor a desert reference: to unhitch my pony from the corral and mosey on down the trail to open territory, then gallop free into uncharted spaces, with only the ever faithful wind of the Spirit in my soul's wild hair. Time for fresh and open terrain, but like so many times before, I had no idea where that might lead. Love reigned and Love won in the end. This was that season of testing the maxim that truth is the twin of love—walking in truth and linking arms with love. When the cup of passive aggressive posture could no longer be contained, the church administrators began a direct approach.

Returning to the church again, when the cup of passive aggressive posture could no longer be contained, the direct summonsing began. These otherwise kind and affable leaders blended into a pallid and pretentious background. I was accused of writing an anonymous letter of character assassination about the offending executive to the elder board. I was fresh out of fight.

My beloved husband, ever championing my causes, stood by me all the way. The overwhelming sadness that engulfed me as I reflected later, was that the most cogent evidence of the utter lack of support for a woman pitted against the system was that there was not one female on the elder board, not one deaconess, no ombudsman of my gender to advocate for me. I was alone. Women are so often alone. Tragically, in Germany it was a pastor's wife who attacked and undermined me. Women do not always support women, either.

I eschewed resentment, though, and refused it a hiding place in my heart. I had paid the price for truth and stood by my convictions. Disapproval and rejection served only to drive me deeper into my Source. Some of the women wanted to continue the classes, and we did just that, meeting in various homes over the next decade. I never dissuaded anyone from staying at the church. Some still are there and also attend my classes.

The gatherings became known as the Lasses Classes and what growth, change, and wonders we women all experienced. Our sequence of studies has been a progression of awareness of union, inclusion, and connectedness. One of the books, *Experiencing the Trinity*, by Darrel W. Johnson, proved to be the most life changing of all the ones we studied; a little book on a massive topic that sealed the love of God forever in our hearts. Countless women have met in morning and evening classes since my departure from the restrictions and restraints of the patriarchy and its constructs.

I was told by a friend that the offending pastor had called me the best teacher they ever had, but that I would not subscribe to the system. Interesting juxtaposition of thoughts! I ached for a place beside my male counterparts for all women. I longed for that elusive butterfly, mutuality.

Storms lay ahead and the flowers began to lose their perfume. The closeness and bonding that all we women had formed, (and that included a book club of about twelve bright and beautiful ladies, now in existence for seventeen years) illuminated the road ahead with their loving support through the darkest days of my life.

When my beloved husband had a stroke, life as I knew it was forever over. Although he was still ambulatory, vascular dementia started to seep through that brilliant mind. The mind that had helped devise computer programs for the defense of the entire free world could now no longer retain a simple password. I had to fall in love with this new Jim. The man I married died several years before he died bodily.

I had massive learning curves to negotiate—to obtain competence in computer technology, for example. Love taught me patience with myself when I was empty of any hope. I learned Christ as my Life as nothing else could ever have taught me. When my grown children, fighting their own battles of loss and dread of death, complained about my sometimes less than honorable and kind behavior, it was the beautiful essence of their father who, unsolicited, called them aside and encouraged them to be patient with my impatience because, "Your mom is afraid." It was his gentle hands that held my face and firmly declared. "I know you—you will chafe under imagined guilt. But I want you to know and remember you are the best caregiver anyone could ever have!" Now *that* is the epitome of selfless love. I still melt in the magnificence of it.

The commitment to marriage when we pledged to erase the word divorce from our vocabulary, was now richly rewarded in an unbreakable bond between two, now broken people. Mutuality had come full circle in my marriage, living proof that self giving love is the only way forward for the male-female stalemate. Jim was known to often say to his married children that to have a successful marriage "You have to die a little every day." His deep love and wisdom still rings true and remains among us.

On another March morning, as the flowers began to bloom in the desert he loved so much, Jim left planet earth for the eternal, endless bloom of heaven. We sent up a bunch of blue and white helium balloons (signifying the colors of the Scottish Flag) into the endlessly clear, desert sky. My beloved husband had taken flight and widowhood had begun.

BOTANICAL GARDENS IN PHOENIX

BRILLIANT ARIZONA SUNSET AND
THE FAMILIAR SILHOETTE OF THE
SAGUARO CACTUS

HOT AIR BALLOONS

JIM
"STANDING ON THE CORNER"
IN WINSLOW, ARIZONA

MONTANA GOLD

Such a silence settles in the fall
    when fields are spent,
    awash in golden glow
    and rolling landscapes rest
    from summer's work.
Through the quietude
    you can almost hear
    a sigh in the stubble—
Relieved of their load of grain
    fields commune together
    in the satisfaction
    of work well done.
A hint of fetid fragrance
    drifts in the stillness.
First fresh snow falling
    on the distant mountains,
    the seal of the season
In rural Montana now.

12
TRANSITION TIME

My first taste of the big sky state of Montana was in our motorhome en route to Alaska from Colorado many years before Jim died. (He was so proud of our Big Foot home on wheels.) I was intrigued by this state's vastness, its variety of scenery and those Island Range mountains. Little did I dream that one day I would have a cabin there and that in the months and years that lay ahead, it would become a womb of gestation that gave birth to a new life. Montana would become synonymous with healing and happiness, lightness and love. Jim knew that our elder son and his wife, Heidi, had bought property near Red Lodge at the north entrance to Yellowstone. We supported the financial acquisition; and, even as he was in hospice care, he dreamed of going fishing in the river that runs through those eight glorious acres. He never did get to catch the big one; he did not even get to see the place; though I believe he did fly over on his way up!

Within a few months of my solo lifestyle, I was ensconced in my beloved cabin, embraced entirely by aspen trees and close to the main cabin where my family lived. There I began to wonder who I was without my husband. Who was I and what was I to do for the rest of my life? I began to write poetry to express my grief. I had gotten my stride as a single woman in as much as I had efficiently executed care of the myriad minutia that are left in the wake of a spouse's death. On his deathbed Jim had rallied briefly in his fading moments of life on earth to ask me, "Are you going to be all right, my darling?"

Well, of course I would be—eventually! But the journey is the story. I am a strong, independent woman in so many ways, and he was my most faithful supporter. He knew, that all my strength aside, I would suffer an irreparable loss in his leaving.

In the cloister of the cabin, its beauty, the well-appointed comfort, the love of my family and miles of wondrous walking, gulping in the breath-taking vistas of mountain ranges, and walking soft meadows, I began to center. Shady Rest (the name of my cabin) for this native Celt, became my Thin Place where heaven and earth come close enough to kiss. It was here in this liminal space that the unexpected, sorrowful news of my beautiful brother's death arrived; a suitable spot of solace from which to field that great loss.

From the fateful night of Jim's stroke, when life lunged sideways, I had wondered where the soundtrack of ethereal heavenly music was ... and where were the slew of comforting Scriptures? In the depths of the horrors of the previous years, I only sensed density of darkness and heard no words of light.

Then I heard the Voice say, "I am *in* you, not just *with* you. I am crying when you cry, sobbing when you sob, and wailing with you in the blackness of bereavement." Then I began to learn what I believed theologically and had taught to others: Union. No daylight between me and the Triune God. That awareness became an inexpressible comfort which assuaged my grief into an anthem, a chant of communion and hope, and a glimpse of going on. My identity is in Christ. Alice is complete in Him, not in Jim, not in marriage or singleness or widowhood. I limped into that growing and expanding happy horizon.

My exuberance for equality, and more so for mutuality, now was subsumed in the transcendent completeness of being one with the cosmic Christ. Gallons of tears watered this seed to fruition, to a semblance of a flourishing flower; searing loneliness leveled and plowed the ground for the planting of the corm; and the courage of conviction propelled me from a fetal position to set firm steps of resolve that opened up undreamed-of new vistas after the anguish of those early days. One tentative step at a time.

MY CABIN DECK IN MONTANA

MOUNTAIN VISTA

MOUNTAIN CATTLE

MONTANA, STATE OF
MANY LOG CABINS

AUTHENTIC LOG CABIN AT
PARIS, MONTANA RANCH

LOVE SECOND TIME AROUND

A man called Ron
   ran a rapid deep root system
   into the ground of my being and
A tree of bright life has sprouted

Kindness and caring are the leaves
   that cover me
Through his strength I am released
   to see and feel again
I am beyond grateful
   outdistanced in delight
   overwhelmed with joy

Even though our leaves are falling
   in bursts of brilliance
The heart is forever young
Love and its attendant lightness
   lusciousness and warm desire
   know no chronology

So till the leaves are gone
   leaving but a skeleton of branches
   that reaches out to the promise
   of perpetual seasons
We will dance as the leaves fall,
   knowing there is forever
   in another form

13
MARRIAGE ONCE MORE

I have noticed a strange phenomenon over the years. Sometimes, the things we never deem possible do occur. That which we are so adamant about, saying "always" or "never"?—well, look out! That I would marry again was one of those *nevers*. I had finally got my muse and method and knew I could make it on my own. Then one day came the text message from my dear friend and student Tori; actually, it came the very next minute after I had just made such a bold utterance to the universe!

"Alice, I'm going to set you up with my lawyer." read the text. Thinking she implied I needed legal help, I responded: "I don't need a lawyer!"

A year and a half later, my matchmaker friend attended our wedding. That he was an egalitarian was an essential; that he loved the same Christ Jesus was not up for debate, but that he was a devout Catholic, would never have featured in my check list, even if I had such a thing!

At our very first meeting, Ron and I spent about two hours sharing the books and authors we both liked. That most of the authors were Catholic did not escape our notice and had been a non-issue for me before; but now, here in the flesh was a papist sipping drinks with me and trying to assess my eligibility as a wife; with me, a rabid daughter of the Reformation!

We were married in the Roman Catholic chapel of St. Francis Savior in Phoenix three years later. There was no Eucharist served, so that my Protestant side of the aisle would not be left out. (This included the bride, who was not required to convert.) This is a fairly recent concession in Catholic weddings of mixed faiths.

In the interest of full disclosure, I will say that I would have settled for a relationship without either the law or the church being involved, if necessary; I would not have categorized this as offensive, knowing it would be decidedly a fully committed, monogamous relationship.

I guess I was wary and weary at the prospect of doing the hard work that marriage demands in order to succeed. I had been there and done that and had lots of T-shirts to show for it. Both the highs and the lows, the glories and the griefs. My beloved suitor would not agree to that, though. In retrospect, I am happy he did not, that I graciously acquiesced and we set an honorable example to our families; though, if truth be told, many of the younger generation have already made their decisions in this regard, and to date have mostly opted for "living together."

Marriage makes more sense from almost every aspect. Certainly, financially. And when we choose to live in the arena of commitment, then change and growth can occur; one can continue to develop both spiritually and emotionally in the crucible of a union. That is the mystery of the church of which marriage is a metaphor.

My new husband had been widowed for eight years and his loneliness and longing for the right one was great. After several failed attempts, he enlisted Mother Mary in a Novena at a certain time in the church calendar. (I think you pay for these things?) He asked her to send him his wife. Rewind to Tori, my friend and his client.

Mary delivered me to Ron within the week. This was amusing to me at first, then I found my thoughts drawn back to the wedding at Cana and how Jesus relented to the imploring of his mother to turn the water into wine! How could I be so sure that she did not continue to have clout?

I felt no direction to deviate to the Roman Catholic lane of faith. Ron was perfectly fine with that. His respect for my integrity speaks volumes to his own security and standing in both his faith, and mine. However, it would not surprise my readers in the least, I am sure, to know that we had some very lively exchanges on the large and the little variables of our beliefs. Some were more heated than others. All were pretty much unresolved and discarded to the slush pile of nonessentials; all that is true and lasting is our oneness in Christ and love, the epitome of that unassailable truth.

As an undiluted Protestant whose sole up-close encounter with a Catholic had been an aunt who converted, I was raised to be kind and respectful of differences. How I simply adore my glorious God! His wonderful ways, His skill in collaborating and colliding with our dogmas and imprinted biases in order to shift unnecessary notions of right and wrong, and particularly to shake Himself free of our ownership of Him. Think of Gideon:

Lord, whose side are you on, ours or theirs?
'Neither, I AM the Lord of hosts.'
(Joshua 5:13-15, paraphrased)

I am also indebted to the Persian poet Rumi, who captured God's grace so eloquently with the quote:

Out beyond ideas of wrongdoing and
rightdoing there is a field,
I'll meet you there.

Ron was an emancipator of all humankind, widely involved in reforms and charitable associations on behalf of the poor and disadvantaged. First of all he quoted, and lived, the continuation of the marriage exhortation (often truncated to omit the husband's responsibility) that reminds the husband to love his bride as Christ loves the church. Even that lesser considered closing command—to submit to one another. Mutuality! He was a tender and fierce fan for my role as a writer, and he honored my womanhood in whatever capacity I chose to celebrate it. I am in awe that I should have been, for the second time around, given a husband with a huge enough heart to cater to the complexity that comprises me. On rare occasions, when he was verging on despair, I encouraged him with the words of my Jim's summation of decades of life with this wife: "Alice is intense, but she is worth it!"

ALICE AND RON'S BELOVED SUMMER HOME IN PINETOP

LOVE THAT WILL NOT

We, and every bird that sings
every blade that brings forth fruit
every worm that burrows in the ground
connected, founded in the desire

of Universal Intelligence
called the Christ
he who loved all into sentience
and proclaimed it sacred and good

tuning the benevolent beating of our hearts
setting the rhythm of every breath
synchronizing every life force to start
and stay, to adapt in awesome array

All creation retains the imprimatur of Love
of a sapience greater than our limitations
Who conducts the orchestra of miraculous grace
in wild beauty of wilderness and restless seas

May we become aware, and face-to-face
with one another, animal, mountain and meadow
behold the wonder of our world hung in space
the value and worth of the broken and bent

And with reverent, tender compassion
love all with the same passion that sent the first cell
into life-pulsing perpetuity; the offspring of divinity,
   of love that will not let go

14
THINKING OUT LOUD

In the lush garden of the home my new groom provided for me, I reveled in nature. He had lived in that place for twenty-six years, and the many trees he had planted during that time were now fully mature. Fig, apricot, pear, peach and plumcot for the picking each in their season. There was also an abundance of citrus trees that could scarcely contain the weight of their bounty; we gave away lemons by the dozens and our glasses of water still always had the addition of fresh Vitamin C in every glass. In the fall, the brilliant colors captured the look of New England, not the desert domain of the Southwest. The wonder of new life stirring, the first sighting and song of returning and nesting birds and the boastful blooming of fruit trees in early spring forever leave me breathless with wonder, love, and praise.

When the searing heat of a Phoenix summer hit, we would take off to the Arizona mountains, to the beauty and bliss of our little summer home, with lower temperatures and afternoon rains that fill the lake and plump happy flowerpots.

These are some of the thoughts and markers of

my life that sail past on the currents of the years … the liminal spaces where I sit, thinking out loud in the company of nature; spaces perched on the threshold of the new, the unknown, between what was and what will be, a place that allows the sacred to settle in the soul.

I recall one such instance some years ago, when I observed the long green grass needing to be mowed in our backyard. I was more captured by the imperative and inspiration that every blade of grass was interconnected with me and with everything else in all creation, than I was moved by the need to mow it.

Similarly, my attention was once arrested in the grocery store when I saw the checkout girl with heaven's eyes. She is included, and she may not even know it! The interconnectedness of all things and the inclusion of all humankind in redemption became the opening chapter of my freedom from religious rhetoric.

I never stopped believing in God (neither has the devil, I am told), but I did not understand or want to know the distant and censorious god of most organized religion. I kept pursuing truth, continuing to readily detect hypocrisy. When, during my nurses' training, a young male Bible study leader had told me I should not go dancing, I suggested he keep a record of his stray thoughts during his evening of scripture study and I would do likewise as I danced to the beat at the Student

Union Saturday Night Ball. I suggested we might want to compare notes as to how innocuous or offensive we had behaved in either thought, word, or deed toward the Lord we both loved. He did not take up my challenge.

The restrictive rubric and the code of behavior so often demanded of followers of the living Christ, seemed completely the opposite of abundant life. It could offer no vibrancy, energy, or freedom to a young, spirited lass from the Isles. So, I went the way of the windswept seas, setting up my sail to leave organized religion dimming to a dot on the horizon and disappearing from my life for many years, indeed up intil the present moment.

Free to be me, just me and not an imitation of anyone else. As Oscar Wilde is reputed to have said. "Be yourself, everyone else is taken." Once I am sure of my Father's never-failing approval, why do I continue to try to obtain affirmation from my equally feeble fellow humans? Because that is the way we are raised from the time we are knee high to a grasshopper. The Apgar score that is applied within five minutes of entry on earth assesses various functions of viability, then renders a score from one to ten. From then on, we are mangled into a meritorious system—from school to college, career, and marriage—and then we reinvent the wheel as we, in turn, rate our children by their achievements. (Of course, you may recognize this trait in grandparents also, although we call it bragging rights!)

Truth is, as a grandmother, though not immune to this weakness, I have done much better with the next generation of my lineage by evaluating them for their innate worth rather than for their achievements.

The living out loud life I now enjoy means being more vulnerable, more transparent, and gentler with myself. During my long history of teaching, I felt compelled to put on my best face, held together with a big Bible under my arm and a smile, praising the Lord though my heart was breaking, and certainly never daring to hint that I lived in anything but the happiest of habitats.

Brennan Manning—a priest and a brilliant writer and theologian—was never quite able to lick his addiction to alcohol. As I watched the movie of his life unfold on the big screen—though I had read just about everything he had written—I collapsed under the unflinching gaze of the same God of Love he knew and trusted. The story shows his wretchedness in the aftermath of drinking. The opening scene depicts him lying in a heap on a New Orleans sidewalk. A young boy comes by and asks him who he is. Not until the end of the movie is the scene replayed, this time with the answer, "I am the man whom Jesus loves!" I wanted to know that kind of assurance more than breath itself.

I began by breathing in and out the unrelenting love of God in every conceivable circumstance. It meant refusing even a whisper of condemnation.

It did not mean I engaged in egregious actions to test that love but, because I did and do and always will fail wretchedly from here till kingdom come whether I like it or not, I need to come to rest in the safety of that acceptance; secure in the outrageous love that would never let me go and would continue to live in and through me no matter what.

So performance oriented was I that learning the lavishness of God's love required simple but profoundly practical illustrations to convince me.

The most graphic teaching moment I experienced in everyday life was so very mundane, but it illustrates the lengths the Spirit will go, to make Love known. I had been hassling with a rather slow and inefficient travel agent all afternoon, and finally my religious façade slipped. I was rather cutting and censorious towards her. Of course, immediately, guilt flooded the system, so an apology to both her and my Lord was quickly out and up, but I felt little relief.

I was scheduled for a horseback ride that evening at my local stable; a long trot and canter through an English summer evening was now blighted by the expectation of punishment. I most certainly could not possibly be assigned my favorite fast horse after such unchristian behavior. Really? Apparently neither God nor the stable owner got that memo; for ride him I surely did.

Doubt and unbelief will never change the facts

of God's unconditional love and His provision for my salvation. That can never be undone, any more than my believing makes it true. I had to abdicate my throne of self-effort, banish from my mind any modicum of merit, and just simply but profoundly become aware of the finished work of Christ, and say: *Thank You.*

It is good to be free of the age-old dread that my prayers are not being heard because of sin in my life or in the lives of those for whom I intercede. That specter of a punishing God is so gone. My prayer posture has changed radically—no bargaining, no pleading, no reminding God of what He should do when I remember that all the promises are YES and Amen in Christ Jesus.

There are many times that I am the answer to my own prayer and that is made very clear if I am listening to directives. I know that whatever happens, all will be well. It remains a mystery as to how it all works, so sometimes I find I am just groaning inarticulately, often with unbidden tears, assured that that is the perfect prayer. The Spirit, the Helper, the Counselor, the Comforter, the Interpreter of the thoughts and intents of the heart comes to my rescue as promised. Thus do I pray for my children and grandchildren, confident that Abba loves them more than even I do! For our wonderful world writhing in pain, I pray in aching wordlessness. And so to sleep, sweet sleep, hurting heart.

SPECTACULAR ARIZONA SUNSET

BOOK SIGNING IN CAVE CREEK, ARIZONA

CARPE DIEM

Living with designed intention
How swift are the seasons. The tension
of time and another dimension
Seizing the day
    not in hedonistic abandon
    but in humble plenitude
In this fleeting gift of time
    there is so much to unwrap
    before the bell tolls
Till it does, Carpe Diem is tattooed on my wrist
    and whispers to live in the moment first

15
TALE *of* THREE TATTOOS

They are tiny; well, at least in comparison to the landscapes of sleeve and body paintings, they are diminutive, and of course, discreet. I have a small symbol of the Trinity permanently patterned on the outside of my left ankle; that was the first one—at seventy years old—the first time I entered a tattoo parlor in my entire life, aided and abetted by some younger ladies with me also getting the same symbol. (Totally supported by my late beloved, Jim; and thankfully, later approved of by Ron.)

The idea was largely born out of our recent study together on the Trinity. The one is an imprint that will perish with the body on which it is painted. The other is an eternal reality of union with the Triune God, which will come to full fruition when the corpus is shed.

The second tattoo is in bold black ink on the outside of my right calf. Reading vertically *l'chaim*, which is Hebrew for: "to life." This one was done a few years later when I was very aware of the rapid passing of time with the accompanying consciousness of the brevity of life and the need to live it fully, without the need for consent or criticism for having another tattoo. Weren't two enough? No, there must be a third; the symbolism of the divine completeness, an imperative.

The iconic actress Judy Dench is one of my great heroines for whom my admiration knows no bounds. When I discovered we both stood no more than five foot three inches from the ground, both challenged with macular degeneration, and that she had her first tattoo late in life, the deal was sealed. *Carpe Diem*—seize the moment—on the inside of our right wrists it was! Surely at seventy nine, seizing every second of precious passing time was the perfect sentiment for my final tattoo.

Everyone asks if it hurts to have them done. My answer is no, but that may be due to the inevitable aging process with its attendant neuropathy, rather than any bravado on my part. What is noteworthy of being age-related is my selection of the location of the sites on my skin. The destinations I determined for my etched artwork are areas that may have ceased slipping and giving way to the downward pull of gravity.

When my youngest son, Ross, noticed that first tattoo he, out of grave concern for his sons, commented "Hmm. What about your grandkids, what will they think?"

So I asked them. Their sentiments? "Nanny, it looks like you are finally having some fun!"

Carpe Diem

FINAL ANALYSIS

If I should fail or fall
   if sheer weariness wins the race
   before I break the ribbon,
   remember me for what I did before I tripped

To finish well is the grandest goal, lest we become
   unknown and unsung
   relegated to the echo chamber of the song
   we once sang so strong

Our deluge of dicta languishing
   in lonely piles and over-full files
   forgotten. That which we so fiercely defended,
   were so sure of, now unread, irrelevant

So quickly one false step sullies a lifetime of labor
   Mercy is in short supply
   to those once loudly lauded,
   who loved so long and worked so hard

An icy aura of abandon envelops the memory
   like relentless waves
   erasing footsteps in the sand
   as the tide approaches

Now to him Who is able
to keep us from falling …

16
LEAVING OUT LOUD

As my journey draws to a close in this form and on this earth, I am overwhelmed with wonder, awe, and gratitude. As I prepare to lay in my oars and unfurl the sail to the winds that still beckon, I am just as excited about living in the closing chapter of my life. I am gratefully in possession of continuing good health and ways and means to enjoy the present moment, drinking deeply of the draft of life, for I know it can change on a dime. I am satisfied and surprised beyond measure at the goodness and richness of my life.

I have no significant wish left unfulfilled. Maybe a few more bucket lists to visit beaches I have known and loved. Of course, I want to stay long enough to see all my grandchildren find their place in this wonderful, though broken and beautiful world; I mean, is there ever a "good time" to go? I told my primary care doctor, in response to her remarking on my healthy constitution, "Well, something will have to come and whisk me away. It is unlikely that I will wake up one morning and just decide it is time to exit!"

I heard of an old lady saying that she would

be ready once she saw all her children safely deposited in nursing homes. That does not feature in my scenario; I want to die before they do, of that I am sure.... Idle talk! It is truly in Another's safe keeping. If one lives too long, then there is that looming specter of loneliness lurking at the door. I have already lost many dear friends who took flight before old age, and the chances of losing even more companions increases the longer one lingers on planet earth.

I am reminded of my perky paternal grandmother who had become very aged. One day, after reading the local weekly newspaper's obituaries and seeing yet another contemporary had died, she took to her bed, face to the wall, in dismay. Her daughter asked her what was wrong, to which she replied, "Why does the Lord not take me?" Despairing over the discrimination in selection for death!

Loneliness is a major player in life, always waiting in the wings, becoming the principal player in the final scene. The reasons are rather obvious and to be expected as one ages.

The loss of a spouse from death I know all too well. Never will I forget the impact of one of the patches on an AIDS quilt that was traveling across the nation at the height of the crisis. An exquisite work of beautiful pieces on a massive quilt embroidered with deeply meaningful aphorisms. This one arrested me: "If Love could have kept you, you never would have died."

Love does not obviate either grief or death. Living in a different location from grown children is hard too. Grandchildren, nearby, no longer need to be baby-sat or picked up from school. Our Taco Wednesdays are over, and I will never again hear my little grandson say, "Mmm. How I love that smell, Nanny!" as I cooked supper for him and his big brothers. Now my cherished grandchildren, with all but two in close proximity, are scattered across the land from sea to shining sea, one actually on the sea as a naval officer on a US destroyer.

Friends die and sickness pays a visit or two as well. Deafness, which isolates you even in the midst of a crowd and you, and everyone else, grows weary of repeating themselves. Yes, there are hearing aids and many of us elders have availed ourselves of their expensive and extraordinary advantages. What others, not so afflicted, may overlook is that one who needs hearing enhancement may also require aids with which to enhance vision, such as reading glasses, distance glasses, and special sunglasses for driving—all of which threaten to dislodge those pricey hearing helps. Add a face-mask to the mix, as was the case during the recent pandemic, and I find myself opting to stay at home or resort back to my quiet world to maintain sanity.

The specter of blindness is a behemoth. I am grateful beyond words for modern medicine that has afforded me the ability to continue to see, despite having two major malfunctions that threaten loss of sight. When I was first diagnosed with both glaucoma and macular degeneration, the prospect was dire indeed. I remember curling up into a fetal ball in the center of my lonely bed in despair and dread. Ten years later, after many surgeries, a million or more continuing eye drops, and direct shots into both eyes every few months or so, blindness has been stalled.

One of my grand boys, when about eight years old, once asked me why grownups were reluctant to tell their age, to which I stuttered, "Well, I guess they don't want to grow old." After a pregnant pause, he replied, "Well that's silly. Everyone, if they live long enough, gets a chance to be every age!" Sagacity beyond his years.

It takes discernment to consider what causes I let consume me. History bears witness that the courage and commitment to challenge the most egregious violations demand sacrifice at every level. Living on a globe that seems to have tilted sideways is disconcerting and screams for my involvement. What has released me to act with acumen and accuracy is coming to recognize much of my disquiet as grieving. I ask myself this question: "What is it that is causing you grief?" When I can identify the source of the pain, then I lean in and listen. From the stillness at the center, I hear this: *Take the colors I have given you and weave them into the whole; from the underside it looks like a tangle of threads, but turn it over and the finished weaving is beautiful.* My particular passion for empowering women is one of the distinct colors I have been given, and I can only trust that I have woven those threads well into the fabric of the whole, that it is taut, long-lasting, and will endure well beyond my tenure here.

It took science to finally gather up all the loose ends, to bring harmony and restoration to my world of thinking, seeing, and doing. Spirituality and Quantum Science have finally embraced; and for many thousands of the disillusioned pilgrims of religion, we have found a resting place.

Indeed, even Quantum physicists admit to "stuttering for words" when asked to define and describe it. That gets me off the hook and allows me to share the effects and influence such awareness has given me—the emancipation, energy, and beauty that this marriage bestows.

Let it suffice to sum up my delight in knowing that scientists in this exciting field agree that there is a world of pure energy, an invisible world that is interconnected; that there is intelligent design and even more, there is undeniable love in that design. This marries perfectly with the truth of Christ. I now see the cosmic Christ has always existed, long before he put on humanity and walked the earth as Jesus of Nazareth. God really did become one of us, no wonder He can comprehend every expression of my humanity—including the wanton, the wayward, and the worst of me.

The company of memories is of immeasurable

comfort. That is why we may be heard reminiscing so much as we get older. I recall my life with poignant gratitude. In the process this serves to assure me that I have lived well, been of value, and fulfilled my calling. It staves off the fear of being alone and the prospect of soon leaving the scene. The company of family is of increasing importance. So don't ever stop calling me, texting me, and picking me up for lunch, my dear family. I am sure you never will.

I have come, most gratefully, to the place of not regretting my past. I used to chastise myself all the time; flogging my foolish, oft misguided zeal and consequent actions that I do think damaged both my marriage and my children for a time. I have shown appropriate remorse; I have never been reluctant to ask for (and receive) forgiveness or make amends wherever possible.

I am fully persuaded that it is in relinquishing pride and presenting myself as vulnerable, that the wonder of unmitigated grace is exposed—that both the prodigal and the self-righteous stay-at-home are confronted with something much more magnificent or egregious than their good or bad works. The relentless love of the Father! In that marvelous milieu of forgiveness and grace, I keenly concur with Edith Piaf when she sings, as only she can, *Non, rien de rien, Non, je ne regret rein!* "No! I regret nothing, for my sin He no longer recalls."

One of the most massive growth curves of which

I am now so blessedly aware at this juncture of the narrative, is that I can trust whatever outcomes ensue for I know the One I trust is trustworthy and is, in totality, LOVE. I can safely say that the spirit-instigated prayer on that straight stretch of English country road is finding fulfillment. It took a close professional friend to observe this reality as she described my writing as that of "one who knows God and does not just write about Him!"

I could not then fully understand just what such knowing would look like. I have since come to understand the words of Jesus in the gospel when He prayed that we would know the Father, which meant an intimacy as in marriage, far beyond mere head knowledge. In other words it has not meant gathering more data on God, but becoming aware of a bride-bridegroom relationship that births divine life in me.

I have told my family that I want to be discovering something new to the very end of my life. I want to leave reading an absorbing book and take flight, proclaiming, "Wow. I never knew that." There will be so very many hands reaching out to greet me. And by the scars I will indubitably know one pair of those Hands above all others!

The OPEN GRAVE

Waves are lapping on the smooth white sands
>he so often strolled

on a day in the budding, promising month of May
>the first green blush on the fields he ploughed

so often
He loved the sound and smells of the living earth
>of the newly turned turf awaiting the seed

A small group of the people he loved
>huddle by the open grave on this May morning

We are bereft

The casket, the dirt waiting to receive the remains
>to cover him in the dark dirt of his island home

Then the larks—a pair of them soaring and swooping—
>trill over the open grave

We lift our heads to see the song
>of a pair of birds, a pair of lovers reunited!

The light of heaven fills our sorrowing souls
>My mother and father together again
>>after thirty long earthly years

EPILOGUE

The same dark water, the crossing always and forever familiar. Long gone were both the open boats and the men who rowed them; now a high-powered ferry fully equipped to carry even cars to the island. This fateful morning, it could not steam to the shore fast enough. As soon as we berthed, I began to run the short distance to my father's little cottage, the wind drowning my wailing.

I loved my dad's hands; those familiar appendages that spoke expressively, that loved excessively, that wrote extensively to friends and family across the globe. Now they lay still across his unmoving chest. When my cousin met Jim and me at the airport, he greeted us with the news that my father had died that morning—a few short hours before we were due to arrive. That morning, twenty-five years ago, I was a fully-grown woman, mother, and grandmother; yet I felt like an orphan.

A few days later we laid his body to rest beside the woman he had loved and lost and lived without for thirty years. The day in May was mild and calm. It was the time of plowing, preparing the land for seed sowing. The fields of open earth around the churchyard represented well the man who loved the soil of his native land, whose gaping grave now awaited his broken body to be planted under the pale blue of a spring sky. In the background the lapping of the waves on the sands he had traversed so often in his 85 years on planet earth, was a fitting anthem for a man of the sea.

First I heard them. Then I saw them. A pair of lavericks (larks), singing, soaring, and dipping down towards the grave together.

Together again; after thirty long years, my mother and father are together again! I heard not another word of the burial service in the churchyard, only the sounds of rejoicing in heaven.

When I had lingered looking at the dear face before the coffin lid went down, one burning question had clamored for corroboration. Do you believe in the resurrection? Do you really believe you will see your father again? Through tears I answered: *Yes, most decidedly I do!*

SHETLAND ISLAND SUNSET

The WIDOW

Becoming a widow
is no small thing
not just the removing of the ring
that has bound
you, that found
you, so long ago

It is surgery sans anesthesia
savage segmentation
cut loose as if in space
weightless and wandering
the familiarity of the earth once known
now hollow, hostile foreign soil

Will a morning ever dawn
that sorrow won't live on
in the rising of the sun?
Tears dry but should flow forever
given the severity of the severance
and the gaping grief of the grave

POSTLUDE

Seven weeks from diagnosis to death. Just about the time this manuscript was ready to be submitted, life launched me into a new lament. My intrepid, robust Ron, husband of almost six years, succumbed to stage four pancreatic cancer.

So, for the second time around, I bear the moniker of "widow." I am alone again. I am thankfully surrounded by a devoted family and faithful friends. But I am still alone. The loss of a spouse is different from all other bereavements because the union of a husband and wife is the fusion of body, mind, and soul, making separation excruciating, as if your skin were ripped off.

The musical postlude at Ron's funeral service was from the symphony "Appalachian Spring," by Aaron Copland, music he so loved. Yes, springtime will, hopefully, come again. In the meantime, I will slowly but surely learn to live in the light of his life, not in the shadow of his death. But oh, I miss those hands. I reach out to touch them, to feel their strength and tenderness …

ALICE AND HER GROOM, RON

Alice's List of RECOMMENDED READING
"Books that Clarified and Confirmed My Evolving Faith"

Giles, Keith. *Sola Mysterium.* Oak Glen: Quoir, 2022.

Johnson, Darrell W. *Experiencing The Trinity.* Vancouver: Regent College Publishing, 2002.

Kruger, C. Baxter. *Jesus and The Undoing of Adam.* Jackson: Perichoresis Press, 2003.

Kroger, Richard Clark & Catherine Clark. *I Suffer Not a Woman.* Grand Rapids: Baker Books, 1998.

Manning, Brennan. *Abba's Child.* Colorado Springs: Nav Press, 2002.

McVey, Steve. *Quantum Life.* Lodi: TWS Publishing, 2023.

Nouwen, Henri J.M. *The Wounded Healer.* New York: Image Books, Doubleday, 1979.

Rohr, Richard. *Everything Belongs.* New York: The Crossroad Publishing Company, 1999.

Rohr, Richard with Mike Morrell. *Divine Dance: The Trinity and Your Transformation.* New Kensington: Whitaker House, 2016.

ACKNOWLEDGMENTS

To all who encouraged me to tell this tale. To those who read the manuscript and gave invaluable feedback: Grant Ferguson, Sandra Trujillo, Marina Mainland Sinclair and Ron, my late husband, who not only gave input and insight, but was ever and always my most ardent fan. And once more, to my most valued editor, Catherine Lawton, and Cladach Publishing for taking another chance on me!

Gratefully I acknowledge the photographers:

> All archive and early family pictures:
> > Sandra Trujillo
>
> Shetland, Ireland, and Yorkshire scenery:
> > Marina Sinclair
>
> Montana scenery:
> > Grant Ferguson
>
> Colorado photos and wedding photo:
> > Alexa Clark
>
> Arizona and Germany photos:
> > UNLEASH
>
> Carpe Diem:
> > Wikimedia
>
> Map of the Shetland Islands:
> > Can Stock Photo / rusak
>
> US flag and Scotland flag:
> > Wikimedia Commons

ABOUT ALICE

Alice Scott-Ferguson is a Scottish-born freelance writer and motivational speaker. Educated as a registered nurse in Scotland, she holds a B.S. in Health Sciences and has worked mainly in the psychiatric field. Contributing to both the secular and religious press, she has authored several Bible studies and prize winning poetry. Her first book, *Little Women, Big God* (1999), tells the story of the women's ministry she founded and directed in the UK.

An engaging and enthusiastic speaker, Alice has traveled internationally, presenting at various venues—seminars, writers workshops, and conferences. She is passionately committed to bring God's liberating love and freedom to her audience. She leads Bible study classes each week locally, and her passion is ever to teach and live out the fierce, limitless love of God.

Her book *Mothers Can't Be Everywhere, But God Is* was released by Cladach Publishing in 2002 and again in 2018. Alice co-authored, with Nancy Parker Brummett, *Reconcilable Differences: Two Friends Debate God's Role for Women* (2006, David C. Cook). Two collections of Alice's poetry, *Pausing in the Passing Places* (2018) and *Unpaused* (2021), are also published by Cladach.

Just months before this book was published, Alice was widowed for the second time. She continues to make her home in Phoenix, close to local family members. She now has four step children and ten step grandchildren in addition to her own three natural children and six grandchildren, scattered across the country. She escapes the desert's summer heat by visiting those of her family who make their homes in Montana and Colorado.

OTHER TITLES
by Alice Scott-Ferguson

available to order through most retailers
and at https://cladach.com/

**Mothers Can't Be Everywhere, but God Is:
A Liberated Look at Motherhood**

Pausing in the
Passing Places:
Poems

Unpaused Poems:
Real, Raw, Relevant

Printed in Great Britain
by Amazon